T0323498

Chaos to Context

This book is your roadmap to successfully navigating your child's middle school years!

Marked by significant physical, cognitive, and emotional changes, this period poses unique challenges that can have a profound impact on middle-grade students' academic performance, social and emotional well-being, and overall development. This book provides the knowledge, resources, and strategies needed to successfully navigate these challenges while creating a nurturing and supportive environment. In addition to covering topics such as puberty, changing social dynamics, identity exploration, digital literacy, and self-advocacy, chapters also provide resources for further reading and reflection questions to inspire dynamic discussion between parent and child.

Parents, caregivers, and educators of middle school students will find the support and guidance in this book invaluable as they help their students foster growth, resilience, and success while navigating this key period of change.

Jody Passanisi has been working with middle graders for 15 years. She is the director of the upper school at Gideon Hausner Jewish Day School in Palo Alto, California, and teaches social studies methods to teachers at Mt. St. Mary's University and Hebrew Union College's DeLeT program. She has written about education for *Scientific American* and *Education Week* and is the author of *History Class Revisited* (2016, Routledge). She advises parents about how to support their children through middle school @chaostocontext on Instagram.

Chaos to Context

A Parent's Guide Through the Middle Grades

Jody Passanisi

Routledge
Taylor & Francis Group

NEW YORK AND LONDON

Designed cover image: © Getty Images

First published 2025
by Routledge
605 Third Avenue, New York, NY 10158

and by Routledge
4 Park Square, Milton Park, Abingdon, Oxon, OX14 4RN

Routledge is an imprint of the Taylor & Francis Group, an informa business

© 2025 Jody Passanisi

The right of Jody Passanisi to be identified as author of this work has been asserted in accordance with sections 77 and 78 of the Copyright, Designs and Patents Act 1988.

ISBN: 9781032864471 (pbk)
ISBN: 9781003527831 (ebk)

DOI: 10.4324/9781003527831

Typeset in Palatino
by Deanta Global Publishing Services, Chennai, India

I hope this book makes middle school easier for someone, be it a kid, a parent, a grown-up, a sibling, a pet, just anyone. A deep and abiding thank you to all three of my children, Levi, Ezra, and Saul, for their existence, as well as a slight apology for the fact that my vocation includes their experiences, at least tangentially. To my middle school boyfriend, who happens to be my husband: Sebastian, as always, thank you for this life we've built.

Contents

Acknowledgments

Thank you to everyone, both those whose names I know and those I haven't met, who made this book possible: Rebecca Collazo and Quinn Cowen at Prufrock Publishing, Philip Stirups at Taylor and Francis, Lillian Woodall, and the editors and typesetters (special thanks to the typesetter) at Deanta, and John Norton and Susan Curtis at MiddleWeb.

A heartfelt thank you to Rose for being there since the very beginning of this project, to Lauren for bouncing ideas back and forth with me, and to Carmen for planting the seed that I could do something meaningful with these experiences. I so appreciate everyone who has taken a moment to read what I've written on @chaostocontext – your experience is my reason for writing about this.

To my dad, who read the first rough draft and all of the drafts I have sent of things over the years. To Cezanne and Becca. To Shara, my writing partner. And to the incredible educators I've had the privilege to work with – especially those who gravitate toward this oft-maligned age group.

I'm grateful for every experience, the middle graders I've known, and to the challenges that have given me the bit of perspective I now hold.

And of course, to Sebastian, Levi, Ezra, and Saul for being my home.

Introduction

On the way to school one morning, my three boys and I (at the time of the writing of this book, two of them have me as their principal, which you can imagine is not complicated at all) were in the car listening to music and I mentioned that I was planning on writing a book about parenting middle schoolers. Child #1 groaned and said, "About *who*? You're *not* writing anything about *me*." (This is dramatic irony, right here – considering I am writing about it right now.)

When I wrote my first book, also about middle schoolers – much more niche – about teaching social studies specifically, I didn't have children in middle school yet. I had middle schoolers that I *taught*. Indeed, I had taught quite a few of them. But I didn't yet have my *own* middle schoolers.

Not to say that having personal middle schoolers in your home in the past, present, or future is a prerequisite for writing about them or knowing deeply about them. I would never say that, nor do I believe that. What I *will* say is that my children have humbled the pants off me. Because I did know a lot about middle schoolers before, and I use a lot of what I've collected in my toolbox while I parent them. And it still is emotional work and I am still exhausted every day.

When I wrote that book, my three boys were five, two and a half, and in utero. So I didn't feel quite up to giving parenting advice, but now, after 20 years in the classroom, and having worked with this age group in both a teaching and administrative context – on top of having a parenting perspective – I feel much more comfortable coming at things from a more holistic stance. One of the struggles of any challenging and intense stage of development for children – and therefore a challenge for parents – is the tendency to focus on the current issue and lose the forest for whichever tree is giving the most trouble at the moment. Zooming out and up to get a bird's-eye view is so important, not just for perspective for *your* sake, but for the sake of the relationship with your middle schooler.

DOI: 10.4324/9781003527831-1

This is the age where you set the stage for the next few years, the years which are going to have higher stakes. The next stage is where communication is going to be even more vital to maintain. If you develop good habits now, you will be in a good place to continue later. In other words, don't play all your cards now. I'm mixing my metaphors here, but it *is* a long game, and sometimes, you need someone to come in and remind you of that when you are caught up in the middle of some middle school crisis.

I started my Instagram account (@chaostocontext) in December 2023 because I was having so many mini-conversations with individual parents both in my office and in my personal life – and the common denominator was me wanting to help them play the long game. Honestly, many times, I felt like I was talking to *myself*. I tell myself daily: "Remember, you're playing the long game."

It's a mantra at this point:

"You *know* better."

"Don't let this phone stuff weigh down the larger picture."

"Is he playing too many computer games? There is a *bigger picture.*"

"This one math grade thing – it's middle school – it's a learning experience – this is a long game."

"This other one said something hurtful – no problem, it's a good opportunity to talk about dignity – no one is perfect."

But it is so hard to do that as a parent and I am not a perfect parent, definitely by far.

People struggle with parenting. *I* struggle with parenting.

It's so much easier to give advice to others than it is to take it yourself.

For example, while I was writing a huge chunk of this book, all of us were home for two weeks of our school's spring break and we were down at the same time with Covid. So the good news was I had time to work on the book and the not-so-good news was that none of us could leave the house. So a couple of alternative titles I bandied about around that time were: "Chaos to Context: or, go play in another room and stop asking me for snacks, I'm writing my parenting book," or, "Chaos to Context: I'm writing a book about middle graders and I can't even get my 14-year-old to leave his room half the time and now he's vitamin D deficient," and my favorite: "Chaos to Context: I swear to god stop hitting each other with those and go find another activity – your mother is trying to write a book about parenting."

So yeah, a good time was had by all. Two weeks with five humans living on top of each other while trying to get anything done is going to stretch the limits of anyone – even though I try to be the best grown-up for my middle graders, or all of my "graders," for that matter.

I love working with middle schoolers because it is my vocation, but that doesn't mean that parenting my own is necessarily easier for me than it is for others. Because there's a lot more that goes into parenting than meets the eye – middle grade or otherwise. There are feelings, emotions, personalities, backgrounds, and traumas – all the things. And so that's why books like this exist – they are intended to help you through those emotional moments. This book is here as an outline for you to go to when you're in that moment where you can't think. The moment when your amygdala is on fire and you don't know what else to do.

Well, here you go, that is what this book is meant to do: provide context for the chaos. Tips and reframing for the struggles. Reminders you aren't alone. Example scenarios just like yours that show you that the thing your kid did last week isn't so unique.

And look – over here! Here is another chapter and *another* scenario that happens all the time – because these children, God love them, are more or less predictable, and thank goodness.

This book will deal with those scenarios that *are* developmentally expected, or within the general parameters, including some unexpected behaviors and occurrences and how to cope with those as well. Very extreme cases are not under the purview of this particular text. This book will discuss the most likely scenarios to come up when you have a middle-grade student: academic, social, emotional, and developmental.

This book will examine the kinds of challenges you expect in puberty, what you expect in terms of friendships, what to expect in terms of what is developmentally appropriate, and when you should be concerned. And when should you ask a psychologist, your pediatrician, or another expert to weigh in.

People always say that there isn't a handbook for how to parent kids because each and everyone is different and unique, but truly there's nothing new under the sun and there's nothing middle graders can't throw us that they haven't thrown at somebody else – the new unprecedented world of technology and social media notwithstanding – so this book intends to look at the aggregate of wisdom from all they've thrown over the years to see what basic guidelines we can use as support through these challenging times. Or, at least, what we can use to keep the drama and histrionics to a minimum. Because the chiller *we* are, the better everything is going to be.

Trust me.

When analyzing middle-grade behaviors, perspectives, and motivation, a lot of the insight I have comes from my own experiences both as an educator and also tapping into when I was a younger person. I have a deep well of empathy for the feelings of middle schoolers at this time of growth and change. I found middle school to be exceptionally painful for many reasons, both extremely internal and expectedly external. I was not particularly well-adjusted or well-regulated and so I can remember, vividly, what it was like to feel dysregulated, but also to make it look, occasionally, like I had it together.

For any parent picking up this book, before you dive into the first chapter on puberty (yes, we are going to start right there because that's where it all happens. Where the "They used to be so (fill in the blank) but now they are (worse in some particular way)" comments arise. So that's absolutely the place we have to start.) I will always have you first search your own feelings about your middle school experience before even *attempting* to address your middle grader's issue because we often project our own feelings onto our children. *Even* if we don't mean to. If our kid experiences a social rejection in sixth grade and they aren't sure how to feel about it, but as soon as they get in the car and share it with us, the story triggers that memory of the time when we walked into the cafeteria with our tray and no one would let us sit with them and we get upset on their behalf and then they raise their response in kind and *voila* – there you have it – an escalated situation. And your kid learned that they should definitely feel bad, even though they *didn't* feel that bad, originally.

But just having painful or challenging and/or great memories of middle school isn't a problem on its own merits. Those memories are a parenting superpower. As I said, I use my memories of these feelings to help my students all the time. I remember what it's like to be confused, to not know what to do to feel like everything is changing and everyone knows what to do but me. To feel like a stranger in my own body, to feel like a stranger in my own life, and in my own family. It makes putting a student's reactions and behavior in context a whole lot easier. And I remember that feeling I had when I was a kid. That feeling that the adult sitting across from me, whoever it was, MUST understand what I was thinking and feeling, because obviously they too had gone through this. It never even occurred to me that they might not remember, might have grown through it *so* much that they'd forgotten how it felt.

That might have reassured me on the one hand, see – "it is only a stage," like they say, but on the other hand, how disappointing, that the people who say they understand, don't really. So try to get back to that place. You don't have to re-feel all the feelings. Just think about who you were and your hopes, how much you understood, how much you didn't understand, and what you wanted. Look through your eyes then. Not your eyes now. And use those eyes to make context from the chaos of what your kid brings you each exciting day of these action-packed four(ish) years of the middle grades.

And do that work first before you start this book:

To start, ask yourself:
When you were 10–14:
Did you go to a school that was K–8 or K–12?
Or a 5–8 or 6–8 stand-alone?
K–8s are often easier to navigate emotionally than stand-alone
   6–8 schools.
Did you move?
Experience a breakup?
Did your parents divorce?
Did you experience the death of a parent? A death of a sibling?
Did you quit a sport or hobby?
Did you start a sport or hobby?

Did you realize you were good at math? Writing?
Did you discover a love of a content area? Science? History?
Did you lose a good friend? Did you gain a good friend?
Were you popular? Were you specifically unpopular?
Were you into something specific?
Did you struggle emotionally/psychologically?
Did you feel bullied?
What names were you called?
What names did you call others?
How did you feel most of the time?
When did you go through puberty?

You might go so far as to write your middle school biography if you feel so inclined. You could share it with your middle grader. But the exercise is mainly for *you*: think about how your experiences affect how you expect to see your *middle grader's* experience. How you react to it so that you can intentionally put it to the side, and purposefully and strategically refer to it later when you need it.

You'll use it when you need to remember how it is to feel like the middle schooler you felt like back then.

But you will go through your memory banks and write your bio now before you get started because right now, they are writing theirs. One of the dangers of parenting is inserting ourselves too much into our kids' bios. We need to be in there enough, but their biographies are for them to write.

For all of the talk about dearths of handbooks on the rearing of children, there have indeed been many many tomes about childrearing over the years. This is another one in a long line. But even though people may say there isn't a handbook, there are certainly innumerable webpages and words spilled about how to do it, how to parent, what *not* to do, what *to* do, such that anyone would feel that, no matter what you do, you are going to screw up your kid.

And you know what? You will! You will kind of screw your kid up a little bit. Breathe and take that in for a second. Because to parent is to accept that. When you first start the parenting journey, if you're anything like I was, you might say to yourself, "But not *me, I* will be different. This truth will apply to everyone else, but me. I will not screw up! I will read everything, do everything, and try my absolute best."

Then, at some point, you realize that you can't control that little human that's somehow been entrusted to you and you haven't slept in days and *you're* human and irritable and perfection just isn't a possibility any longer. And you know what? That's good because the expectation of perfection is not fair to you and most importantly, it's not fair to your kid.

Realizing that you're not the perfect parent and that you'll screw up your kid (again, not a lot, a *little*) allows for real moments of connection, allows for humility, allows for the space for you to meet your kid where they are. And it is really, really important for this stage of their development to meet them where they are. Because the middle-grade stage is messy and if you can't be a little bit messy too – if you are still clinging to the hope that you are going to be that perfect parent – then they aren't going to feel like they can relate to you.

Being an imperfect parent comes with perks. It allows you to model essential skills for your middle grader, essential skills they need to get through these years:

- ◆ Humility
- ◆ Acknowledging mistakes
- ◆ Apologizing effectively
- ◆ Coping with adversity
- ◆ Managing anger
- ◆ Navigating upsetting situations
- ◆ Lifelong learning
- ◆ Engaging in self-reflection
- ◆ Embracing community responsibility
- ◆ Cultivating empathy

That feeling of needing your kid to be perfect and needing to be perfect yourself are certainly possible contributing factors to the rise in anxiety that adolescents are experiencing. In fact, adolescents with an anxious parent are three times as likely to experience anxiety themselves (Ross). With all the information out there, it's much more likely that each piece of information contradicts itself, leading to confusion, informational whiplash, and a feeling that each parenting choice one makes is vital and pivotal, and the outcomes, whether negative or positive, could affect a child's life trajectory and choices in an outsized way.

This anxiety is the seed of fear, love, and hope for our children's future from which helicopter parenting fomented. This is the desire for our children to lead lives without struggle, pain, and heartbreak from which snowplow parenting came into being.

But these parenting styles are stymying our children and unfortunately are working at cross purposes to what they are purporting to combat.

Each parent's hopes for their child are unique. But what their child actually *is* and will *be* is shaped by their own experiences, who they are, the world they live in, and the choices they make. They will need to be equipped with tools and skills – like resilience, empathy, self-reflection, and self-regulation – to get through this world as a person. And the middle grades are when they start becoming the person they are going to really be. So this is a book for parents who are ready to support their students and help them go down the road of becoming the person they are going to be.

But first, you'll need to give up the castle in the air where you and your child live in perfection. It's a wonderful thing to give up. It's freeing. It's beautiful. It will be a gift for you and for your middle grader.

This book is intended to be a support for you as you go through this stage with your middle grader: a guide to know what is expected, a guide for when you should intervene, a guide for when to let things play out (or let things play out and *then* intervene), and ultimately, something to help contextualize what can seem like a whole lot of chaos out there. And not just the chaos of middle-grade development, because at the end of the day, it's not *actually* chaotic, it's predictable, it goes according to plan, albeit not always super linearly, but also the chaos of emotions and reactions and feelings and worry of "Am I doing enough?" "What if I don't step in? What will happen?" "What *if* I step in? What will happen?"

It might *feel* like chaos, but this book will help, one chapter at a time, to make context out of the chaos.

You don't have to be perfect for your middle grader. You just have to be the grown-up. Because they will be going *through* it.

Now, on to puberty.

1

Spoiler Alert: It's Puberty. Puberty's the Problem

Personal Inventory

When did you go through puberty?

◆ Early?
◆ Late?
◆ When "everyone else" did?

On a scale of 1–10, 1 being not at all and 10 being a great deal, how self-conscious were you about your changing body?

1 2 3 4 5 6 7 8 9 10

Puberty: A Cruel Irony? A Celebration? Or Both?

It can seem a cruel irony that the same time humans become overly conscious of how they look compared with others is the same time they lose full control over their bodies due to hormones and the changes of puberty.

DOI: 10.4324/9781003527831-2

No kid feels about puberty one way. I remember I couldn't wait to get older and go through all the milestones, but then when kids started making fun of me for having an "overdeveloped" chest, I hid behind my books and binders for three years until everyone caught up. If your kid *seems* unfazed, they are probably at least a little bit fazed. If they seem fazed, there are parts of puberty that probably rolls off their backs, too.

All that to say, we are *meant* to be a little bit fazed. After all, who wouldn't be? During these years of middle school, kids grow an average of 8 cm in height each year (Reese) – but never at the same time or the same speed as each other. Everyone's faces are changing, hair is erupting all over the place, and feelings, emotional and physical, stronger than they've experienced since they were toddlers, have taken hold – sometimes with or without tantrums. Meanwhile, the expectations and responsibilities around them have ramped up in intensity and the result is that everything can feel out of control. But, it bears repeating, *never for everyone at the same time.* Every middle grader is almost always on a slightly different page, so there's lots of variety in growth and development to witness in your average middle school classroom.

So, let's start from the beginning of puberty. What happens? Why does it happen? And more importantly, what are the impacts of these changes on the lives of middle graders? Is puberty what's to blame for the bad rap that middle school gets? (Spoiler alert: yeah, kind of.) All of the physical changes come with hormonal changes which come with emotional changes which in turn affect relationships and social dynamics, family dynamics, and self-esteem. Once we delve into all of the places into which puberty has dug its tentacles, we will talk strategy: what now? How can parents help normalize the changes, beyond what is covered in sex-ed in the middle grades – and help your middle grader put their feelings in a right-sized box of containment so that it is something manageable. So that you can build resilience, develop rapport, and create trust around challenging communication topics that will serve you and your middle grader well as these years unfold.

Remember, before you delve into this cesspool (just kidding!) (sort of!) of puberty, do an inventory of your feelings about your growing up. Remember the facts of it, how you felt about it, what you wish were different – take stock of it because an unexamined middle school experience will seep out to your kids in ways you might not expect, notice, or want. Did puberty go OK for you? Did you come out relatively unscathed? Was it traumatic? Did you feel like you developed too soon? Too slowly? Were you worried about a particular part of your development? Your body? Your height? How did you look? More importantly, how did you FEEL you looked? How much time did you spend thinking about it? No time? Some time? An inordinate amount of time? An embarrassing amount of time? Did your parents or grown-ups ignore the changes happening to you? Did they pay TOO much attention to your changing body? Did you have conversations with trusted grown-ups that helped you to feel OK in your own body even as things changed?

That is the goal: the change is coming, whether it's happened for your kid already, whether they are going through it right now, or whether they've passed through parts of it, it's coming. The key is that they know about it, can contextualize it, know there is a spectrum and extended timeline for that development, that they have someone they can talk to about it, an adult or close peer or both, and that they feel like they can handle most challenges and mood swings that they inevitably experience around it. They are going to have these challenges. But the hope is that, with some reframing and help from you, they can sit with and contextualize their feelings a bit better than a raging toddler in a supermarket who can't have that candy bar.

The Difference

Because now it isn't quite enough to just remember how we felt. Our kids have a lot more pressure now. When I was growing up, parents were concerned about the pressure of fashion magazines and the unrealistic standards they set. The examples of heroin chic led girls, specifically, to hurt their bodies to maintain a standard impossible to achieve. Now, the pressure to look a certain way is everywhere – the Internet tells us that there is one way to parent our kids, and it tells our kids there is one way to look.

And that is not a great message during puberty.

The Body

Puberty could be classified as what the philosopher Mircea Eliade called a liminal space. Not quite one thing and not quite the other. An in-between moment manifested physically, kids are half-angles and half-rounded, they are tall, but also not tall, one part of their body seems large and another still small. This is not a great time to be told that to be worthy of love one must look a certain way.

In puberty so many different parts of the body are changing, it's enough to give us perspective as to why things might feel out of balance.

Students must even get used to the sounds of their voices again, as students' voices change – and, not just students who were born male as media would lead us to believe. All students who go through puberty experience voice mutations: male voices drop about one octave, and female voices drop approximately three to four semitones (Zamponi et al.). By the end of puberty, kids have a different voice from when they began. It's not just different tonally, it's got a different structure physically. The vocal folds are changed, the larynx moves, and the sound that comes out, well, it's a whole new thing.

For anyone who has listened to themselves on a recording of any kind, the shock of hearing one's voice can be jarring – add to that the changing nature of the voice, changing at this rate, with these physical characteristics and accompanying feelings, and there is another aspect of puberty to contend with.

Hormonal changes are a large contributor to the volatile and cyclical nature of mood and emotion during this time of rapid growth and change. The limbic system is activated, receptors bound by increases in estrogen and testosterone, stimulating sex drive, physical and also emotional feelings, and intense feelings – love, lust, and desire. These new sexual feelings and the accompanying emotional feelings can lead to volatile behavior and impulsivity on the part of students, often without their understanding of the root cause (Breehl).

A Disconnect

Puberty is the process where a human person physically develops and sexually matures to the point in which they can reproduce (Breehl). Putting this in stark terms, this brings the disjointedness of puberty home, as both a parent and an educator. We are talking about students who range from about ten to 14 years old – students who are going through this process and who are experiencing the hormonal and physiological changes that prepare the body to reproduce, but in a society where they are not expected socially (not just "not expected" *really* not expected), not emotionally ready, and still, in essence, practically children in the bodies of reproducers. This is the disconnect we face. I think about a class of fifth graders and it's a STARK disconnect. These are not humans ready for that particular stage of life. And yet physically, they've been given the tools:

> Just because kids look more sexually mature doesn't mean they want to have sex. Our society has long conflated the onset of puberty with becoming a sexual being. Which is fair, because the path to sexual maturity does, indeed, include the emergence of sexual urges and desires. But with the earlier start to puberty, for many kids beginning around fourth grade, the onset of puberty and the onset of sexual activity are no longer in sync. They never were, really – sexualization has a range just like everything else that occurs during adolescence, and it evolves not just because the body parts develop but also because the maturing brain, soaked in the hormones controlling puberty, guides it to.
>
> (Natterson and Kroll 7–8)

It is super cool that growth happens! Growth is expected and part of the process of being human. But we wouldn't have angst around transitions, change, and this particular growth period if there weren't some difficulties associated with it. This stage happens so quickly if you think about it. In the same way that a teeny baby went from bopping around with no neck strength to speak of, to dare-deviling themselves every which way on the playground as a toddler, to working on fine-motor skills in kindergarten – fifth graders to eighth graders (approximately) go from the latency stage to full-fledged adult animals with sexual potential in about four-ish years – which is truly, an incredible transformation.

But our society and how we function as human beings are slow to account for this transformation. If we were to have a more aligned society, our ten- to 14-year-olds would begin "mating" and start procreating at the end of this puberty period once they were ready. But that's not the way our society is set up, nor is it the way the human brain is set up to handle things. They have the physical tools but lack the emotional toolbox. So as grown-ups, we must first contextualize and grasp this change ourselves, understand the physiology behind puberty, and the physical changes that are happening, and then it is much easier to remind ourselves what kids are experiencing.

The Changing Body and Shaky Positive Self-Regard

In this world of filters and constant monitoring of others' activities and curated lives, it is unsurprising that the normal stages of puberty and development would exacerbate an already fraught time and make it even harder for middle graders to develop positive feelings toward their bodies. There has been increasing research showing a positive correlation between social media use and increased body dissatisfaction, eating disorders, and suicidal ideation ("Exploring the Effect of Social Media").

Some challenges can be anticipated: of specific concern to males can be the appearance of enlarged breasts at this time. This is called gynecomastia of puberty and is a benign condition that results from a temporary imbalance between estrogen and testosterone production (Breehl). However temporary this might be, it can cause concern for boys, especially if they aren't expressing the concern, thinking perhaps that it is 1. NOT benign 2. Permanent 3. Just them.

The above example represents one of the most important reasons to keep an open dialogue about puberty with your middle grader. They may not want to speak with you about it and that is fine. But you want to make sure that they have *someone* they can speak to about it. And at this age, it's OK to be stealthy. Leave an article about gynecomastia or puberty out where they are sure to find it, but not so much that they think you left it for them. Or just be direct: say, "You know, when I was your age, I worried about _____. I wonder if you are worrying about something. I just want you to know I am here to talk about it with you. Also, these changes your body is experiencing, many of them are temporary.

All of these things that students might experience for the first time – some may be upsetting to them and some of these changes might not faze them at all. Don't be surprised if what fazes them isn't what you expected. For example, the issue *au courant* in my middle son's fifth-grade classroom is height. Anytime I hear them talk to each other, they are jockeying to sort themselves according to height. There are no other categories right now that matter.

But next year it could be something else. The fascinating thing about these four years is that it's all going to happen pretty much at some point within the span, but never for the same kid at the same time. Whether it's acne, widening hips, a developed chest, a perceived underdeveloped chest, a surprise erection, a wet dream, a new sexual fantasy, or a thought that makes them uncomfortable or guilty, feeling like they are growing too much and too fast or not enough and too slow, it is going to take open dialogue and communication to help them to understand that this is truly a physiological, temporary, and survivable process. And yes, it IS a process to celebrate! How exciting that the body can do new things. How exciting that it has skills that it didn't have before. But it is a bit nerve-wracking at the same time. For students, and parents as well.

If it were just about managing feelings, physical and emotional, about the changing body, the chapter would end here. But it's not. All of these changes affect other aspects of a middle grader's life, from their friendships to their home life. These are the pieces that are more individualized, and unique to each kid.

Friendships

Friendships are fluid in the middle grades. If you think about it, it makes sense. The friendships are fluid because the students change where they are in their developmental journey several times and those times that they change don't always correspond with the stages of the friends that they currently have. For example, Charlotte and Lena have been friends since kindergarten. Their parents are friends, they do EVERYTHING together. They've hit fifth grade and all of a sudden, Lena has started freezing Charlotte out. Charlotte feels hurt but doesn't want to make it a huge thing so doesn't say anything. When it's time for her birthday, her mom invites Lena without talking to her about it and is surprised, not just by how Lena looks, but by how Lena talks to Charlotte – like she's a baby, and like Lena is much more mature. Charlotte's mom is upset. She thought they would be friends forever.

Sound familiar?

This is not a friendship that is destined to never return. In fact, once Charlotte goes through her own maturity growth spurt, she and Lena can reconnect again, if that happens to be in the cards, which is more likely the less grown-up intervention occurs. So, I would tell (non-existent) Charlotte's mom to just wait the whole thing out.

For one, while it doesn't seem like Charlotte is THRILLED with Lena's behavior and low-key snubbing, she's clearly not dis-traught. She has other friends. Sometimes parents will project their own stuff onto this kind of thing and Charlotte will come away feeling worse than she did before. Lena is, as we say in the middle school business, "GOING THROUGH IT." Through it being, puberty – the change. And that is expected. Now, if Lena says something awful or nasty to Charlotte then there's cause to intervene in some way, but right now, this is an example of two kids being in two different places on the developmental spec-trum even though they are the same age and in the same grade.

And this is the fluid bit. Kids' grown-ups get concerned about their kids' peers. And rightly so. Peers at this age are really important. That being said, friends one day are not always friends the next. So approach with caution. Don't react right away. Wait and see if it is a thing. If your kid is chatting with someone you aren't thrilled about but it's only been a week, wait and see if it lasts. And wait and see if your reasons for not being thrilled are valid. Kids are often pretty great on the inside, once you get to know them. Also, they're kids. They are still not baked yet. Give them time.

And if you insist that your kid continue a friendship they've clearly outgrown, or if your kid is grieving a friendship that has been outgrown, there's not necessarily an actionable item for you. You can be there, you can listen. You don't have to do anything. Kids will learn from this that they don't have control over every-thing, but that is OK. You don't want them to come out of middle school feeling like they need to control people. But if they come out feeling like they have self-control, that is definitely a good thing.

So when it's time to worry about whether your kid is in the same class as their best friend or not in the same class as their nemesis, remember that those roles may not be the same roles two months into the school year as they are right now. Everything changes. Everything is temporary. This is good because it means that if things aren't going great, it'll change soon! Challenging in that, in a time of change, this is another place where change can add to the weight they are already carrying.

Family Dynamics

While there are changes in how your middle grader will interact with family, this one bastion can be a place of significant stability – as much stability as possible. It's not like you can't move cities, or houses, or separate from a spouse or partner – and certainly you can't control things like illness, food insecurity, or loss. But you can control what you *can* control. The more stability you can provide on the home front, the better. Things can get a bit, well, chaotic, in a middle schooler's body, brain, and feelings, and when they know they have a place of stability to come back to, they can be more grounded, more resilient, better able to work through the challenges that are thrown at them. This also means that they might melt down for you. And if things are externally hard to control, you can control your temperament, you can stay calm. You can provide your middle grader some calm in a tempest-tossed sea.

Just like your toddler would melt into your arms into a massive tantrum when you picked them up from daycare, your middle schooler, if they know you'll hold their anger, their difficult emotions, their sadness, and their fear, they will bring it to you (Arky). It might not look so neat and tidy as that. It might look more like "Mom, you never let me ___ I HATE YOU." But, you have to learn to speak middle schooler.

More on how to speak middle schooler later.

For this chapter, it's important to know that the routines of home, the habits, and stability are good – when possible. Family game night, dinners, donuts on Sunday mornings, cooking a meal together, going for a walk, movie night with popcorn. Whatever you do and have time to manage, keep doing it. They may not WANT to do it, but once they are there, they will appreciate that it's something somehow immutable, even though everything else seems to be shifting under their feet.

They may want to spend more time alone, in their room. They may want to spend more time online, gaming, texting with friends – depending on the norms and rules of your home and what is allowed, and at what age. But there must be times with family, painful as it might be to pull them out at first. They will warm up. And you might not have a kid like that at all. Temperament and introversion/extroversion tend to ramp up here. If you've got an extrovert kid, they may not have this issue at all.

Romance and Relationships

Some kids will be slower to develop romantic/sexual feelings, some might not be activated in that way at all, and for some kids, this time period might be a burgeoning of intense sexual feelings. The body is getting ready, even if society isn't set up to make that happen. Kids this age, despite their growing understanding of sex and the feelings that go with it, can still be emotionally immature and are often not ready to actually have a romantic relationship. It's totally normal to not have romantic feelings in middle school. But some kids do and embark on a relationship – that, at the least, can be emotionally intense. Usually, these relationships tend to be just talk, perhaps some hand-holding, some kissing, some a bit more than that. While there haven't been many recent longitudinal studies at the publishing of this book, in 2014, Rice et al. found that about 5% of adolescents had sent or received a sext, which is very likely the more likely outcome for current teens to move toward, considering their predilection for texting in lieu of more face-to-face interactions. And while done in 2010, a study conducted among middle schoolers found that 9% were engaged in oral sex/sexual intercourse.

But it's as important, if not more important, to minister to your student's emotional needs in terms of their romantic relationships at this period in their lives.

Don't diminish their feelings as "just a crush."

I don't know about you, but some of my most significant heartbreaks happened before I turned 20. Even middle graders are capable of intense feelings and of course this corresponds to their sexual awakening.

Listen, approach with curiosity, and don't react too much – either with concern or excitement. Some kids might want to talk about it endlessly and others might not want to talk about it at all.

Make sure they've had the sex talk – see Chapter 5 for more info on this. Discuss your expectations and boundaries around this. It is not out of the realm of possibility that your middle grader could hold hands, and kiss – but more than that is likely more than they can handle emotionally at this stage of development. Let them know what YOU expect.

Remind them that you are here to listen. Follow up if the relationship continues. Ask them about it to make sure that they are treating each other respectfully and respecting each other's boundaries – emotional or physical. You also want your middle grader to know they can come to you when things go sideways. There will likely be a breakup somewhere – and the first one can be hard. They might want to share. Or they might not. But you can be there for them. Make sure to remind them these feelings are strong – but they will not always feel this way.

This kind of relationship is a unique learning experience, and you can't protect them from the learning – or prevent them from having feelings for someone. But you can support them through it and make sure they know their worth is not just tied to this relationship or their relationship status.

Gender

Gender and biological sex aren't the same thing. Gender is how someone feels on the inside, and sex is the biology a person is born with. Sexual orientation is who that person wants to hold hands with/is sexually/romantically attracted to (Sexual Orientation and Gender Diversity). The kids in this generation have very little issue in differentiating this and the relationships between students of all types and permutations of the above are played out in the middle school arena and beyond. Most relevantly for this chapter, students who are transgender, especially those whose families are concerned about interventions, have an added concern about puberty affecting their preferred gender expression (the gender that they look like on the outside). This can be very complicated and is best discussed with a professional. LGBTQ+ students, especially students who are transgender, have high rates of suicidality, gender dysphoria, and other negative outcomes. Indeed, 82% of transgender youth have had thoughts of ending their life (Austin et al.). Seeking support for your middle grader, regardless of how supportive your community or family is, can go a long way to mitigate these outcomes. Lisa Damour, PhD, writes in her 2023 book, *The Emotional Lives of Teenagers*:

> Should teenagers express an interest in biological interventions – such as taking medications to suppress puberty, undergoing cross-sex hormone treatment, or having gender-affirming surgical procedures – families do not have to weigh these complex decisions alone. Many communities have university-affiliated clinics with departments that specialize in caring for gender-expansive teenagers….Your second job is to protect your working

relationship with your teenager. The best approach is to treat your teenager as the driver of their own gender car, with parents viewing yourselves as loving front-seat passengers who are along for the ride.

(70)

Hygiene, It's A Whole Thing

Hygiene, but Make It Fun!

The props of puberty were one of the things that made it fun.

When I was still far beyond needing it, I remember looking at the kids in the Clearasil commercials and thinking that they were so cool to even be at the stage to NEED something like that.

Be careful what you wish for.

But the products intended for tweens and teens are designed, in theory, for their unique needs. At the very least, the products are eye-catching – so that they will buy them and want to use them. So, capitalize on that and make it fun for them. Whether it's deodorant or shampoo, let them choose the color and style they want. If choosing products is not their jam and when you ask their preference they look like a deer in the middle of a CVS, then give them a choice between two options.

If you want to go fancier, the kids love Sephora and Ulta these days. One of my coworkers and I recently were hanging out with our kids and eighth-grade international exchange students (boys) who were here for a week. The boys wanted to go to Sephora while they were visiting. One wanted to get his sister a particular Drunk Elephant product, and the other one wanted a particular cologne for himself. So if you can't beat them, join them. It's the middle way of hygiene. Do you want your student to go on an endless quest for the holy grail of glass skin? Of course not. That isn't healthy, and in middle school, well nigh impossible. But giving them some agency, and choice, and putting some fun in the whole process isn't a bad thing either.

You will need to show them, as Vanessa Kroll and Cara Natterson explain in their book *This is So Awkward: Modern Puberty Explained*:

We adults have been washing our bodies for decades – trying new products, changing habits, getting to know what works and what doesn't. Kids are total novices here, so they need very specific instructions like Wash your body with soap or even Wash your armpits, penis, feet, then tush with soap. Don't assume they know any-thing—remember this is still the kid who poops, doesn't wash their hands, then walks into the kitchen and grabs a handful of tortilla chips. They need detailed, step-by-step instructions, and some need it written down and taped to the bathroom wall.

(91)

As with everything, talking about these things is really the key. Help them by acknowledging that this time IS awkward and that it IS absolutely normal to have these feelings of not being sure about whether they are growing too fast or too slow, or whether they look right, or whether they have too much hair or not enough hair. There isn't any person on this planet who is fully satisfied with how they look and certainly not during puberty (Natterson and Kroll, 108).

Hygiene and Morality

Hygiene is a neutral concept, but our choices about hygiene can have moral implications. Throughout history, we have assigned moral values to aspects of hygiene, such as how much hair we have and how we manage our "basest" bodily functions. These moral values are often based on cultural beliefs and norms, and they can vary widely from one society to another.

Values about hygiene are often based on the idea that certain bodily functions are dirty or shameful. But what our bodies cycle through, grow and do, produce, and get rid of are things that tie humans together across time, space, and distance. They are a part of our shared human experience, and they are nothing to be ashamed of. For a middle grader, these messages are important to get at home because they will very likely not get them from a larger peer group.

And they are experiencing some of these things the body can grow and do for the first time, so even though whatever they are experiencing has been happening since humans were a thing, they may worry what is happening to them isn't normal.

Remind them that it's not only "normal," it just IS.

It doesn't have to be good or bad. It just is.

And, there is a fine line between health and hygiene. Some hygiene choices are for health, not just for appearance's sake. And that line isn't a solid one. Putting lotion on ashy elbows and knees can be important because skin health is important – not just because of appearance.

Learning to wash properly in ALL places isn't an appearance choice, there are health imperatives to keeping areas clean – avoiding bacterial and fungal issues that can happen.

But in terms of whether your middle grader wants their hair a certain way, or doesn't want to get rid of body hair, while you can allow or not allow those choices as the parent, try not to put a value judgment on them.

This is super easy, right?

Hygiene, Meet Social Pressure

Other things will come up. I remember the first time my mother told me about how to bleach my lip hair. It was in middle school. Before she mentioned it, I didn't know it was a thing. She had good timing. I don't remember getting teased for it, and I got teased for a lot of things. Your kid may not want to, indeed, may *choose* to do less maintenance. Either way is fine. But the conversation is key: you don't want your kid making a choice they don't actually want to make because they were teased, and you don't want your kid being teased because they didn't know that they *had* a choice.

It's hard to look at the dynamics of this age and think: Why are human beings like this? Belonging, for one. People badly want to belong, and conformity, or at least conformity to certain criteria, is often a prerequisite to belonging. And norms: there is such a spectrum of consciousness of hygiene and awareness at this age, the peer group is the thing that helps move the needle closer to the middle – in theory – to balance.

Is there a peer who doesn't smell good? You can be sure they will tell them. A kid who has hairy arms? They'll tell her, too. Why? Because *they* aren't sure it's OK. And by mentioning it, they are testing it, moving things more toward vanilla. More toward what they think "normal" is.

The issue is that no one ever gets to the center, to normal, to the middle, to perfect. That's why this age is so hard. For them, and you. Because there is a lot of contextualizing you will need to do.

Reframing and Right-Sizing, Dare I Say, Contextualizing?

Whether it's hygiene difficulties, friendship challenges, romantic relationships, or body image, with what they bring, you will likely be either minimized or maximized. Students rarely hit the right target in terms of right-sizing their concerns and issues, and, of course, they wouldn't. This is the first time they've really become aware that they HAVE concerns and issues and that they have a modicum of autonomy and responsibility in solving them themselves. It's that last part that is one of the most exciting parts of raising a middle grader. Because they can do so much more than they were able to before. Not only are they able to perceive things, abstract things, new ideas, problems, challenges, and feelings that they weren't able to previously, but they can work to solve them. They can use their nascent tools to practice being a person in the world. Middle school is the perfect place to practice. Not all the parts are quite put together the way they will be at the end whether it's parts of the body or parts of the brain (more on that in the next chapter) so there's some hit or miss happening here. But all that hit or miss, the practice, the growth, the trial and error – it's all building resilience and a feeling of self-efficacy in their own physical and emotional body – a feeling that they are a person who is competent and able to move about the world. As a person, we are both body and self. Puberty separates these two things and in middle school, the process by the end is to reintegrate them back together into identity, a cohesive whole, a self. But to do this, students need grown-ups along the way who will help them right-size. They need their grown-ups to be grown-ups. Remember, they are the ones going through a bunch of physical, hormonal, emotional stuff. The adults need to be, as much as possible, the ones to help reframe. That modeling is how they will learn to, eventually, do that for themselves.

Downsizing

Sometimes parents are surprised that their kids don't know how to right-size their problems already, on their own. Most people don't! They haven't practiced. And if you watch, people are really triggered by certain emotional situations, and those kinds of situations happen *all the time* in middle school. For example, exclusion, unkindness, shaming, and loneliness. So grown-ups, don't take the bait. It seems like they WANT you to react with heightened emotion. It may even seem like when you don't they are disappointed. Just because they want you to react in a certain way doesn't mean it's the correct reaction. We make the mistake that just because our kids are suddenly able to write essays and do algebra and logically argue with us sometimes that what they want must be the correct thing. It's not always. They don't always know what they need. They are full of puberty and hormones.

They need right-sizing.

Sometimes that's just nodding and listening as they share their feelings with you. This is the time to ask: Do you want me to listen, or do you want me to help you problem-solve? This is a phrase that can be used for almost EVERY conversation. Sometimes we assume they want us to step in – and we feel like we aren't "doing our job" if we don't, but they often don't want us to and if we do we aren't letting them figure it out for themselves.

Sometimes just listening right-sizes the problem for them. They've processed it by sharing it and now they can see it more clearly. Sometimes, they need you to ask questions. Often, without meaning to, the grown-up's questions can trigger the student to get more upset. *"What* did she say to you?" "Did she say that to anyone else?" "Did anyone *else* have to do that?"

Instead, focus on actionable items: "I wonder what you can do next?" "How will that look tomorrow?" "What will you say to her next time you see her?" "What can you control in this situation?" "What can you do right now that will help you to feel better?"

To have them focus on their next steps, ground them in reality, and take them out of perseveration, they can focus on what they can do and what is in their sphere of control. They will also see that you take their feelings seriously, but that you don't think their situation is the end of the world, which will be a relief. They don't want it to be, either.

Sometimes, less often, but sometimes, they need someone to raise an alarm. I've had a kid come to me a few days out and tell me that a friend of theirs said they were thinking about ending their life – and, "Is that something I should tell someone about?" There have been a few times when, as an administrator, I've had to tell students that they SHOULD have involved an adult in the conversation a long time ago.

At some point, you have to have a conversation with your kid: there's always a tipping point. There are ground rules: If someone is in danger – to themselves or others, or if someone is hurting someone else or getting hurt – that's automatic grown-up involvement, for whatever the situation calls for. And that's how life works. It's not about "getting in trouble," which is what they are usually worried about. It's about getting help for whoever needs it, which is much, much, much more important. Always.

If a student is worried someone is going to hurt someone else or themselves. If someone is being hurt by someone, if they think something just doesn't feel right with an adult, or if they are just wondering if they should tell someone something, have them tell you to test to see if it is "a thing."

The idea is: if they tell you and it's not a thing, hooray! It's *not* a thing! But if it IS a thing, then good thing they came to you. It's a win-win. Then, this is the time where if they say, "I don't want you to problem-solve, or I don't want you to tell someone," you have to say, "Remember those ground rules? If someone is in danger to themselves or others? Or if someone is getting hurt? I have to step in. It's my job."

But most of the time, they need you to help them to lower the hyperbole. To provide some perspective, to ground them in time, space, and context.

Not Just Puberty

That puberty stuff. It's tough to know where they are going to be from one moment to the next. From the hormones to the body changes and how all of those affect mood, relationships, and self-image, you'd think that would be enough, but the brain plays an important role, too, in the growth of middle schoolers and their holistic development. That's where we'll go next. Onward! To the brain!

Talk Middle Grader to Me: Chapter 1

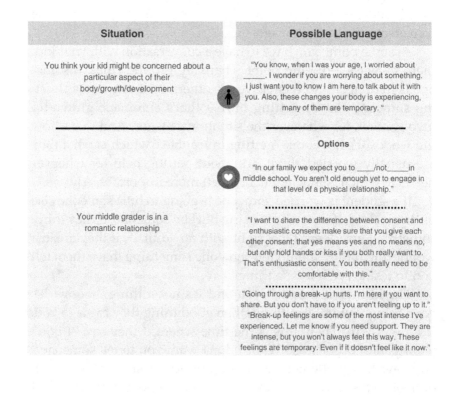

Situation	Possible Language
You think your kid might be concerned about a particular aspect of their body/growth/development	"You know, when I was your age, I worried about _____. I wonder if you are worrying about something. I just want you to know I am here to talk about it with you. Also, these changes your body is experiencing, many of them are temporary. "
	Options
Your middle grader is in a romantic relationship	"In our family we expect you to ____/not____in middle school. You aren't old enough yet to engage in that level of a physical relationship."
	"I want to share the difference between consent and enthusiastic consent: make sure that you give each other consent: that yes means yes and no means no, but only hold hands or kiss if you both really want to. That's enthusiastic consent. You both really need to be comfortable with this."
	"Going through a break-up hurts. I'm here if you want to share. But you don't have to if you aren't feeling up to it." "Break-up feelings are some of the most intense I've experienced. Let me know if you need support. They are intense, but you won't always feel this way. These feelings are temporary. Even if it doesn't feel like it now."

Situation	Possible Language
Active listening for when your middle grader has an issue and you are trying to help them right-size it	"Do you want me to listen, or do you want me to help you problem-solve?"*
Downsizing a problem and helping them to regain locus of control	"I wonder what you can do next?" "How will that look tomorrow?" "What will you say to her next time you see her?" "What can you control in this situation?" What can you do right now that will help you to feel better?"
At some point, probably around third grade, and repeated any time your kid shares anything important with you, you need to reiterate your guidelines for confidentiality/privacy: These are Ground Rules for what constitutes a THING:	"If someone is in danger— to themselves or others, or if someone is hurting someone else or getting hurt- that's involvement, for whatever the situation calls for. And that's how life works. It's not about "getting in trouble" which is what they are usually worried about. It's about getting help for whoever needs it, which is much much much more important. Always."
Your middle grader says "I don't want to get anyone in trouble"	"It's not about getting someone in trouble, it's about resolving a situation, helping someone, or helping people repair this relationship."
If they tell you that they don't want you to problem-solve or tell someone and you need to Upsize their issue:	You have to say, "Remember those ground rules? If someone is in danger to themselves or others? Or if someone is getting hurt? I have to step in. It's my job as a grown-up." This is what we call a THING.

2

Unveiling the Adolescent Brain

Personal Inventory

Try to remember what it was like when you were nine. How much did you understand about the world and your place in it when you were ten? How much agency did you have when you were 11?

Try to remember how conscious you were. When did things change? *What* changed?

Was there a catalyst for the change?

Were you an emotional middle schooler?

Did you feel like you were angry a lot?

Did you take everything personally?

My main memory of becoming conscious was receiving my first-semester report card in sixth grade. Until that very moment, it didn't occur to me that my effort had ANYTHING to do with the grades I earned. This might sound ridiculous, but this is not uncommon at this age. Middle-grade students' brains develop concurrently with their bodies, and very helpfully not at the same time or rate, and both slowly and somehow all at once.

DOI: 10.4324/9781003527831-3

So when I received this report card, I thought to myself, "I could do better than this. If I did…stuff…would that make a difference?" So I tried the next semester and put effort into my school and homework, and it actually worked. My next report card looked much closer to my perception of my own abilities. But I had to make that connection in order to see those results.

It isn't uncommon for younger students to connect their marks or achievements to their perception of the extent to which the teacher likes or dislikes them. For them, there isn't a connection between their output or effort and the result. This is developmentally appropriate. This connection is abstracted, and why grades aren't particularly effective for students in the elementary grades. For middle-grade students, in my experience, grades are effective only to the extent to which students can figure out how to calibrate their effort to the result. And this concept of calibration is a complicated matter requiring a great deal of executive functioning skills, high-level connections, and abstract thought.

So it is not a surprise that students, especially early middle graders, find it challenging to do some of the executive functioning required of them with the increased workload of middle school academics (which will be discussed in more detail in Chapter 6). They have not yet, or have only recently, become conscious of the connection between their agency in the whole matter in the first place.

All of this is to say we often expect our middle graders to arrive at fifth or sixth grade and immediately be up for the challenges set forth for them, but their teachers know that it will be a process. And for some, it's *not* an easy process. This is often due to the way the brain develops at this point. It's more of a brick-by-brick situation than an unveiling – happening bit by bit and piece by piece. There will be no panacea that will make it easier. The process of learning will be the teacher.

Think back to yourself at this time: how much can you remember? Are your memories hazy? Do you remember "having it together"? When did things "click" for you? Keep all these memories in mind as you go through this chapter.

First Things First: Who Are the Players in Cognitive Development?

To get a sense of the scope of what is occurring in the brain during adolescence, beginning around 11 years old, one needs to familiarize oneself with the players in the game. The MVPs, the ones who show up again and again in the processes that, again, run concurrently with all that puberty stuff, that make for a very interesting few years, indeed.

The Prefrontal Cortex vs. The Reactive Brain

The brain is of two minds: the prefrontal cortex vs. the autonomic brain/reactive brain. Seventeen percent of what we do is controlled by the prefrontal cortex, and that particular part of the brain is not yet fully developed in middle graders, nay, won't fully develop for a while yet, though it is making *some* strides during the middle grades (Wolpert-Gawron). This is the part of the brain that controls all the control-ly type stuff. The stuff that we often bemoan that our kids aren't always great at or aren't *consistently* great at: organization, executive functioning, keeping track of their stuff, remembering to turn in their homework, making good decisions, judging whether something is wise to do or try, and taking another's perspective. And no wonder, their brains are still building the system to support these skills. So they need to be taught and they need a lot of practice. The prefrontal cortex, since it hasn't been developed, is incredibly vulnerable to being hijacked by emotions and hormones, and that is why middle graders' grown-ups' job of reframing and helping to right-size their challenges is so very important.

If you are reading that number above, 17%, and thinking, "Hmmm, 17% for the part of the brain that governs self-control, that is not a very big number," you're not wrong! And, think of it as, in actuality, even smaller, because again, it's not yet fully developed in our middle graders till much later. Of course, it's not *exactly* 17% percent, there is a range, but 17% is a good way to remember how little of our actions are controlled by this part of our brains.

At this stage of development, our kids are going through what Damour calls a "major neurological renovation" and it's not happening evenly or at a measured pace. And, while it is happening at the same time as puberty, it's not going to gift you with the convenience of the same challenges at the same time. First, the changes will occur in the automatic regions of the brain before they even touch the more sophisticated prefrontal cortex (Damour, 78).

The automatic system, the reactive brain, or the limbic system is what governs the more, let's say, emotional and motivational responses. Our feelings and responses, fight, flight, fawn, freeze – fear, anger – are all parts of the limbic system (Shapiro). And, well, the limbic system works just fine in middle schoolers.

This is the part of the brain that served our ancient ancestors well. The ones from which we got this early timing for the onset of puberty and the need to run away from a woolly mammoth without overthinking our escape options. The prefrontal cortex, capable of complex reasoning, is very good in the situations that middle schoolers will be thrown into, and the middle school climate favors students who develop this savviness, especially the social piece of it, earlier.

But there are advantages to the reactive brain, the limbic system: for one, it's literally life-saving (modern woolly mammoth situations), and two, it allows for quick thinking, even thinking based on emotions. That is the purview of the amygdala. The amygdala knows you better than anyone. Your amygdala has been paying attention to everything and knows how to respond. It doesn't have to think, it can just FEEL. You could say it's a best friend – your, sometimes histrionic best friend.

The Amygdala: Your Most Histrionic Friend, and Its Chiller Friend, the Hippocampus

So, sometimes the amygdala is *not* your best friend. Sometimes the amygdala makes it very challenging to think clearly. It wants to REACT. It wants to react so BAD. It's that friend you have to pull back in a fight pretty much every time it gets into it.

My children are probably tired of my saying, "Take some deep breaths. Your amygdala is probably on fire right now so it's going to be hard to think. Let's think through this once it's calmed down," but I find that it is a particularly helpful way of reminding them that their feelings are currently taking over. I think it helps to anthropomorphize the amygdala a bit because it's been my experience that when kids realize that the feelings they are feeling are a result of something either physiological or neurological happening to them, they tend to feel a little less out of control, especially if you can assure them it's a temporary feeling.

But because your amygdala is in charge of responding to stimuli and specifically NOT spending time evaluating, because it's part of the limbic system, the automatic brain, it isn't *evaluating* whether or not the stimuli are an *actual* issue.

This is where you can have a very upset kid who needs their problem downsized. But their emotion is *absolutely* high level. And so they won't be able to think through any right-sizing process with you because they are hijacked by their automatic brain.

This is one of the reasons why your middle grader might not tell you the truth about a situation. They might come home and tell you that "such and such" happened – to find later that the incident was much less intense or less hurtful toward your kid than they portrayed it to be. Partly this is human nature; we like to look like the protagonist in our own stories. But also, if your kid's amygdala is super activated and in super fight mode, then they may very well have experienced that event in the heightened way they described, even though it was not, in fact, or reality, that way. In their mind, they aren't lying, per se, even if they have hyperbolized events – they are matching it to the intensity of their feeling.

But, again, not to be a broken record, this is why our kids can be unreliable narrators. Not because they are untrustworthy or unreliable as a rule, but because their brains are developing and working in such a way that their emotions are driving a lot of their narrative, not necessarily their judgment. And this makes sense when you go back and think about the 17% number (that's really much lower for them).

You might say, we all have an amygdala, why is it so active during the middle grades?

Great question! Well, first, puberty. It's always puberty's fault and the hormones and feelings, and all the things. But, also according to a study by Pfiefer and Blackemore (2012) cited in Robinson (2017), not only is the amygdala's sensitivity increased during this period but there are also increases in the ventral striatum, which plays a role in dopamine, learning, and mood (Haber). So dopamine, that shot of good feeling a middle schooler gets when they hug their grown-ups, hang out with their friends, score a goal in soccer, get positive feedback in class, and do a physical activity they enjoy – all these also play a part. This can be why students of this age find video games and game-based learning compelling, and also why they are at risk for certain risky addictive behaviors if they are not under grown-up monitoring (Semrud-Clikeman).

The hippocampus and amygdala are also very tied together in the learning process. Our emotions can sway our thinking, but, to the same extent, our thoughts have the ability, when used prudently, to calm our emotions. The hippocampus, which plays a big part in learning and memory, is right by the amygdala, and that relationship between emotions and learning can be leveraged quite a bit in the learning process (Jensen et al., 100). It's a relationship to lean into and to capitalize on, rather than bemoan. Middle graders can be emotionally activated and interested quickly – mysteries, learning experiences with real-life implications, and things that matter – social justice and works for the community can be leveraged to make meaning for students and benefit the larger community. I will discuss this more in Chapter 8.

Synapses, Neurons, and RAS, Oh My!

Piaget and Abstract Thought

The ability of a middle grader to all of a sudden think abstractly feels like it happens overnight. Many years ago, Jean Piaget created a still-used theory of cognitive development that organizes a child's understanding into different periods: the two that are relevant to middle grader development are the concrete operations stage, which, according to Piaget, is from approximately seven to 11 years old, and the formal operations period, which begins around age 11 (Scott). As we've seen above with development in the brain, this theory corresponds with gains in the development of the prefrontal cortex of middle-grade students. While Piaget's theories were developed in the 1930s, they are still taught in child development and psychology classes and are in use today.

For our purposes in this chapter, it is important to connect the abilities of middle-grade students to developments in the brain and how everything is working alongside hormonal changes.

The inferential abilities of middle-grade students, which are all part of Piaget's theory of cognitive development in the formal operation stage, are part of what is possible after the changes in the brain. A middle grader can now observe, extrapolate information, and infer and theorize in a way that they weren't able to do before.

Building and Rebuilding Brain Connections

All of this is awesome. Suddenly, you have a kid who can hold a much more nuanced conversation with you about complex topics. They may not yet have the background knowledge to substantiate all their ideas and claims, but the brain of a middle grader is so much more CAPABLE than it was before. And now, not only can it think more complexly, and abstractly, but because of the shift from rote learning to inferential and abstract thinking, along with the neuronal pathways of the students, AND all the synapses that run between them as a result of chemical changes, students are primed for learning.

All of this is then picked through by the Reticular Activating System, the RAS, and stored in long-term memory. This shift in focus is supported by the increased connectivity in the brain and by chemical changes in the neuronal pathways that support both short and long-term memory (Semrud-Clikeman).

While the brain is being rehauled, all of the neurons and the synapses that run between them are running like mad in the cerebral cortex. They get continually sheared away when they are no longer needed, the RAS helping to discern what is important to keep and what can be tossed (Semrud-Clikeman).

OK. OK. So What Can You Expect When You're Cognitively Developing?

Unlike puberty, none of the changes in the brain can be seen in the physical body. Some of what ends up being markedly different in a middle grader's life was alluded to above – specifically the complex reasoning piece and the effect of the amygdala on emotion, mood, and learning, but there are other very important ways that the brain changes during this time end up affecting the experience of middle school and the middle grades.

Complex Reasoning and Abstract Thought

The Amazing Things They Can Do!

Middle graders can be really fun to hang out with. You can watch a movie with them and discuss it afterward. You can read a book and discuss the characters and themes. You can talk about politics, history, things that you believe in, songs you like, art, or anything of interest. They won't always want to talk with you. If you have a particular type of kid, you might need to carve out time for them to be tricked into doing things with you, but most middle graders still really value one-on-one time with a parent or important grown-up and will go along with what you propose if it means they will get it. These conversations that they have with you can be interesting, because they may start professing different opinions than you, which is a whole other thing, and I will discuss that more in the next chapter on identity formation.

In school, this newfound ability to think abstractly means that they can do higher-level mathematics, they can make inferences from primary source documents in history and discern the bias of historians, infer the properties of a substance in chemistry based on its behavior in an experiment, look at literature symbolically and pull out language that is figurative to show what an author is conveying to the reader through its use. It looks like ramped-up academics that might be daunting and challenging at first. It may take a while to get used to these nascent skills. But ultimately, these skills are really about using the brain, and the parts of the brain that are creative – the ones that are used to make meaning.

Disparity Gaps and the Brain: We Need Brain Ed

In my experience, one of the challenges of teaching this age group is that in any given class, especially in grades 5–7, there will be a mixture of kids who are still in Piaget's concrete operations stage. This means that they are strong logical thinkers, good at summarizing, and learning things by rote, but abstract thought is a basic ability for them until they get to the formal operations stage. This is often why things click for students later in high school, or why certain subjects were challenging in middle school, but easier later.

So what does this mean? It might mean just…waiting it out. The challenge, in my experience, is keeping the love of learning in a child who feels like they are getting the feeling that they "aren't good at" something because their peers have developed faster than they have. The class you are in within the US school system is based on the timing of birthdays, but when you are a kid there is a wide range of age from that year in the classroom *and* a wide range of development between students *despite* age.

If there is anything we've learned from the puberty chapter, it is that this stuff doesn't happen for everyone at the same time. So neither does it for the brain stuff either. If you are a middle schooler and your friend is, say, in Honors Geometry because they hit formal operations in seventh grade and killed it in math, but you just didn't yet, you might feel now like you, well, suck at math.

Think about it: there could have been a "Sliding Doors" situation where you were some famous mathematician but lost interest and passion because of the timing of when you reached formal operations and when you took geometry vs. when your friend did. This is not ideal. For the child or for the world.

And, how to mitigate this is a challenge, because schools can absolutely feed into the narrative that early and faster achievement equals better and smarter. Sometimes it is true. Sometimes it's not. Usually, the kids who are in the higher-level classes do better; it's the ones who aren't that need the assurance that they are by no means less than others. Learning is just not a race. Or it *is* a race, but it's a marathon, that goes on for your whole life. It's not a sprint.

Obviously, as with most gaps of this nature, it is much more pronounced with students who are members of already systemically challenged and lesser-funded groups and institutions – students of color and/or low socio-economic status, feeding into the cycles of poverty and preexisting education gaps, making it harder to make gains generationally. We need to do better for children. All children. But we can focus on the ones who aren't getting what they need; the ones who are getting the messaging that they can't, that they aren't good enough.

We don't do an *amazing* job with puberty education, sharing with students what happens to their bodies during the middle grades and all of the hormonal changes and what exactly will happen to them – and especially sharing with them about the normal range and the amount of time it takes for all this to happen, but we do teach it. But we DEFINITELY don't share enough with them about what happens to their brains at this time.

Child development majors, teachers, and psychologists all study formal operations and know that it can take time for a middle grader to get there. They are familiar enough with the brain to know that students' prefrontal cortex, that 17% of the brain that is in charge of self-control, empathy, and reflection, is growing, slowly, they also are very familiar with Carol Dweck's research out of Stanford about Growth Mindset (Armstrong), and that has definitely been shared with middle graders. But we haven't put it all together for the students. We haven't shared with them that their brains are growing, slowly, at different rates. We haven't developed a Brain Ed curriculum.

The following things are true:

◆ The body changes between 8/9–14 at different rates.

◆ The part of the brain called the prefrontal cortex begins to develop at this stage. This is the part that controls, well, all the control stuff: executive functioning, self-control, empathy, self-regulation. It isn't even *close* to being fully developed by the end of middle school.

◆ Formal operations, the cognitive developmental stage where students move from more logical and factual understandings to more abstract and inferential ability, begins during the middle grades. This doesn't happen for everyone at the same time. There is a range. It BEGINS around age 11.

◆ A growth mindset is based on the idea that we can learn new things and new skills, which in the middle grades couldn't be more true – remember all those synapses and neurons going to town, building new information and skills, there's nothing "fixed" about acknowledging and developing skills in the middle grades.

◆ The middle grades are full of change. They are for learning about the self and others. They are for growing. They are for transformation: physically, academically, socially, and emotionally. And it doesn't happen all at once and it happens at different times for everyone and it doesn't make anyone better than anyone else.

◆ AND knowing all of this is important. *Believing* it is.

And, knowing all of this isn't going to fix everything. Even if every kid took a class and learned all of it. It's not going to fix everything. Because the mess is kind of part of the learning. A critical piece is the individual resilience your middle grader develops by going through it.

Though it would be great if they did learn this. It's not going to fix it, but it certainly wouldn't hurt. Some schools do this. Many districts do this. But brain ed isn't widespread in the way puberty ed is.

I know enough about middle schoolers to know that everyone learning this is not going to 100% fix relational aggression. It's not going to fix someone bragging to another that their test score is better, or that they are smarter because they are in a higher level of math, or because they can do something so-and-so cannot. But what it can do is equip you, the parent/grown-up, and your middle grader with the information, tools, and language to at least know the truth about the brain. That yeah, it's going to take a hot second. And so be patient. And let the haters hate. And it'll all sort itself out in the end.

Social Dynamics and the Brain

Let the haters hate.

That's awful advice.

Who said that!?

Don't let the haters hate, especially in middle school. In fact, let's get down to it. Let's talk about middle school social dynamics. This section will specifically address social dynamics in terms of how they relate to the brain. Chapter 5 goes into more detail about social dynamics in broader terms.

Cognitive functioning plays a huge part in middle-grade students' awareness of their social dynamics. Middle school girls are about two years ahead in their intellectual and cognitive abilities, which looks like getting better grades, and, usually, hitting that abstract thought faster. Girls are also hitting puberty early and so are bigger and more capable physically. Because our society puts great stress on boys needing to feel and look successful and capable in comparison with girls. This can create tension between boys and girls and the resentment can create negative cycles of interactions that form the basis of toxic relationships between the genders that continue as the students age (Damour, 66).

Whether you have a girl, boy, non-binary, or non-gender-conforming child, it's important to help them change their language about their value relative to others. If you hear your child put down another child based on their gender/sex, or really anything else, then it's time to reframe: remember, this is something that will be hard for a middle grader. This is prefrontal cortex stuff.

The putdowns might not have to do with anything tangible. They might just be unkind. You might need say in response to even a whiff of unkindness from your middle grader – even if that unkindness is coming from a place of insecurity:

- ◆ "In our family, my expectation is that we don't say things that might make someone feel bad."
- ◆ "In our family, we don't make comments about how people look or say things to people about what they can't change."
- ◆ "In our family, we judge people based on what they do and how they treat us and this doesn't sound like that."
- ◆ "We respect each other's differences. Let's aim to do that next time."
- ◆ "It's important to our family that we use language that recognizes and respects people's differences. Let's be more mindful of the language we use."

Some of this might need to be even more direct. We are dealing with middle graders.

This sounds very Pollyanna-ish, but it is a habit that will serve them well going forward.

The habits they develop now will be the ones they take to high school and college.

If they roll their eyes at you in middle school, it's fine. Let 'em roll. But they will still hear you say it, and hear you. They'll hear you say it later when they are thinking about doing that same behavior. It helps them to think twice before they speak. It doesn't always stop the speech, but it usually helps to bring about a pause, at least.

Kids can be mean in middle school. They have the language to do a lot of damage and the social savvy to pull it off but lack the empathy to put themselves in others' shoes or really look at the long game. Their prefrontal cortex growth isn't keeping up with the social milieu.

There are more connections between the brain and social dynamics. For students who don't feel they have social status, there is a correlation between that feeling and a reduction in their gray matter. Feelings of social isolation also diminish the production of new cells in the region of the hippocampus which, as we saw above, affects learning (Jensen et al.).

Social isolation, even the perception of social isolation, affects their learning.

Now you might say, which is it? Are they supposed to be *resilient*? Or am I supposed to come in and fix it if they are hurting because of social stuff? Because that learning thing pushed a button. I get it.

You definitely don't just let the haters hate. But not because you need to save your kid, necessarily. It's more for the good of the ecosystem. The good of the community.

Because the haters, in this situation, are just middle schoolers, like your kid. Their frontal lobes aren't developed either. They are doing their best too. In my experience, kids think they are good people, they think they are nice people. So it's really important, actually, for students to advocate for themselves and speak up if there's a social issue.

Now, you might say, my middle grader *tried* that and there were social ramifications. I get that too. The school has to handle it properly. The students need someone to sit with them and mediate, to walk them through perspective-taking. But I believe in middle schoolers. I believe that perspective-taking is hard for them (because of all the brain stuff). And they will do better if they KNOW BETTER.

A lot of students also say they "don't want to get anyone in trouble." But going back to the chapter on puberty, it's not about getting someone in trouble, it is about repairing a relationship. The relationship is already cracked. There's already trouble. Now it's time for repair. And that can't happen until your middle graders share with a trustworthy adult.

Back to the stepping-in question: do you need to step in? It depends. Is there a trustworthy adult your student can go to at school? Is this a school thing? Or can your kid solve it on their own with their friend? Is it internet-based? Do they want your support in how to respond? Ask them, but have them take the wheel. They can be a student driver. You don't want to grab the wheel from them while they are doing OK.

Focus, Concentration, Sleep, Physical Activity, and the Brain

To be able to *steer* a car, even with a trusted adult helping out in the passenger seat, your middle grader needs to be able to focus, a skill that has been increasingly challenging for students. I am not here to discuss the use of medication in dealing with challenges of focus, though as an educator I have my own experiences with it, but rather to explain the role of the brain in focus in general at this age.

Ironically, because I just spent a whole section talking about how to calm the amygdala DOWN, focus can sometimes be about ramping that section of the brain up a bit. That's why the hippocampus and amygdala, the emotional and learning sections of the brain, are connected: to really connect students to material, to grab them, and sometimes get them excited about a historical mystery or what will happen in a science lab or the next part of a book or what the symbols in a poem might mean, or in what ways their work can have a real-world impact – all of those things can help to make learning meaningful, thus improving focus.

There are a number of things that are helpful for focus and concentration for students, one being physical activities. It is both helpful in the short and long term. Students in the middle grades often have less physical activity during their recess and lunch times, though they do participate often in after-school sports. Physical activity before a task can help the brain focus, and sustained habits of physical activity help even more (Jensen et al., 113).

Sleep is vital for middle graders in order to help them DO all the things that they need to do to grow. By this point, it should be clear how many moving parts we're dealing with and each plays a really important part. For example, the RAS plays an important role in deciding what to keep in long-term memory storage. It also plays a role in REM sleep (Arguinchona). Nothing works alone. Everything is connected. Kids six to 12 years of age need nine to 12 hours of sleep and teens 13–18 need eight to ten hours. The prevalence of short sleep duration among middle schoolers was 57.8% in a study conducted in 2018 (Wheaton). This is significant not only because lack of sleep leads to poor physiological, emotional, and academic outcomes, as well as declines in student mental health (Wheaton), but it also, as one can imagine, helps to inhibit the parts of the brain that are responsible for control – the prefrontal cortex, thus increasing risky and unreflective behavior.

Lack of sleep leads to poor choices. Many students in middle school are staying up late, texting with their friends, playing video games, chatting, watching something, doing homework – but it's vital for middle graders to have a solid bedtime with time for screen detox before it.

Having a set bedtime for your middle grader is important. Unless you have middle graders who put themselves to bed early, this is a decision you must make for them. They are not mature enough to make this decision for themselves.

What Do All These Brain Changes Mean for You and Your Middle Grader?

The middle grades are, well, in the middle. Sometimes your middle grader will seem exceptionally mature, and the next minute, the next second even, will seem like they've regressed into a first grader. It's fascinating, expected, and all part of the process. They are still kids, but they are getting their adult "stuff" – brain stuff, body stuff, hormone stuff, all the stuff – a little at a time and, of course, never at the same time or same rate.

They do have the capability to think quite logically, and, if they want something (or don't want to do something), they will attempt to outlogic you every time. And, once they get to formal operations, they're capable of abstract thought. But they aren't always capable of sound logic, and their logic is tied up with a lot of emotions and not a lot of life experience. So what does all this mean for you and your middle grader? It's not like every time you're frustrated with your middle grader you're going to go straight to brain science to contextualize it, though that's not a bad idea. But there are a few places where their abilities to reason and their nascent prefrontal cortex come into play – this section will touch on those instances specifically.

What Decisions Are Appropriate for a Middle Grader to Make?

All of that to say, they can reason pretty well, and they crave independence and autonomy (more about that in the next chapter), so it is imperative that they have a voice in decision-making with the stuff that isn't non-negotiable.

Which decisions they can handle depends on the kid. What non-negotiables are for your family is up to your family. You might have a kid who is good at moderation, good at balance, so they can decide when they go to bed, for example. There should be a discussion, and there *need* to be parameters. Then, they can choose options within the parameters.

As a grown-up, you are in charge of setting those parameters. You've built the plane (I know, we were just talking about student drivers and cars, but strap in, we are moving to the sky), but your middle grader can roam about the cabin, as long as the seatbelt sign is off.

But you can't expect them to know how to pilot the plane or navigate the route yet. They just don't have enough experience, training, practice, or neurological development to have that kind of responsibility.

You can't even rely on them to *tell* you if they are ready to make a big decision. By design, they can't always gauge what is right for them. That's why they have *you*. The grown-up.

What Decisions Aren't Appropriate for a Middle Grader to Make?

Generally speaking, parents seem to be giving their kids a lot more say in their life choices than they had themselves when they were growing up. This can be very empowering for middle graders. They can choose whether or not to try something, like which sports or extracurriculars they want to pursue. This is why decision-making, especially the kind of choices that involve many possible outcomes and that require modeling of different scenarios, isn't their forte. For example, where and whether they go to school isn't something a middle schooler should have full say over, or how much screen time they have, whether they get a phone or not, whether you monitor their messages, or when they go to bed, or whether they brush their teeth or bathe. These kinds of decisions are beyond their developmental level. Can they give input, and be involved in the decision-making processes? Of course!

Adolescents, according to brain scans, make their decisions by relying much more heavily on the emotional regions of their brains as opposed to the prefrontal cortex when compared with adults. They make decisions based on their "gut feelings" (Arain et al.).

Sometimes by allowing middle graders to make big decisions, we think we are handing them the freedom of choice, but that choice may be too much of a burden since they don't have the perspective, experience, or maturity to hold it.

Parents may be scared of hurting their kid's feelings or upsetting or disappointing their kid. So it's easier to give them the reins. That way, the decision is *theirs* – the only person they can be mad at is themselves. But this can actually be quite anxiety-producing for the child, because, yes, your middle grader *is* still a child, mature though they may act (sometimes). It's worth it to take a step back and remind yourself that angering your kid by creating a boundary about something that needs to happen or not happen is you being the grown-up. And that's actually what they want. They want there to be a grown-up.

They don't want to have to be the grown-up.

Balance: Boundaries, Risk, and Realistic Expectations

Risk is a concern at this age. For all the reasons that middle graders can't make big decisions about their lives, they tend to make poor decisions about risky behaviors:

> The adolescent years are a time of self-exploration and risky decision-making (Reyna & Farley, 2006). Most teens' risky decisions can be explained by the delayed maturation that happens in the prefrontal cortex – an area of the brain known to manage critical thinking, responsible decision-making, and anticipating consequences of choices. This part of the brain is not fully developed in teens and can be impaired even further by the high emotions that dominate the life of a teen.
>
> (Jensen et al., 141–142)

An adaptive reason for these risky behaviors is the move from dependence to independence – from being dependent on family, to emotionally relying on peers. More and more, at this age, students will gravitate toward their peers for support and validation. Risky behaviors that attract the adoration and attention of peers serve to move the attention from the home to the peer group, thus hastening the individuation process (Riedijk and Harakeh).

It is very important, as it is to have conversations about puberty and the brain, to have conversations about risky behaviors: sex, drugs, and alcohol. Despite the young age of middle graders, especially early middle graders, these topics are relevant and important, and as a result of the Internet, these topics, whether they understand them or not, are ubiquitous. I will discuss ways to have those conversations with your middle grader in Chapter 5 in the "How to Talk to Your Middle Grader About_____" section, so whether in the car or in the air, fasten those seatbelts!

This age is a dance between give and take, independence and dependence, privileges and responsibilities, empathy and selfishness, and reaction and reflection. Your middle grader needs boundaries that grow with them as they do. Their brain is growing up and you will be both proactive and reactive by:

Asking questions if they seem upset:

- ◆ "What could you do to help move the feeling through your body?"
- ◆ "Tell me about it."
- ◆ "Let me know if you'd like me to listen or help you problem-solve."

Setting boundaries when necessary:

- ◆ "In our family, going to school isn't optional. Let me know if you want me to take you or Mom."

Helping them to advocate for themselves:

- ◆ "It sounds like things are getting worse with your interactions with Ella. What do you think a next step could be that would help move things toward repair?"

Reminding them of empathy:

◆ "In our family, we use our words to lift people up. Today your words hurt Jason. How will you help him feel better and repair the relationship?"

Middle graders are learning, throughout these years, that instead of lashing out, or saying something mean, there are better ways of managing – that is what developing a frontal lobe is all about, learning adaptive behaviors, seeing the world from the perspective of others and learning how to relate to other people (Semrud-Clikeman). But they need to both learn and practice these skills. Sometimes it might feel like you are practicing it ALL THE TIME. But never fear, one day it'll click and they'll be onto another skill soon. Remember, it's a long game and they are learning to become themselves.

Talk Middle Grader to Me: Chapter 2

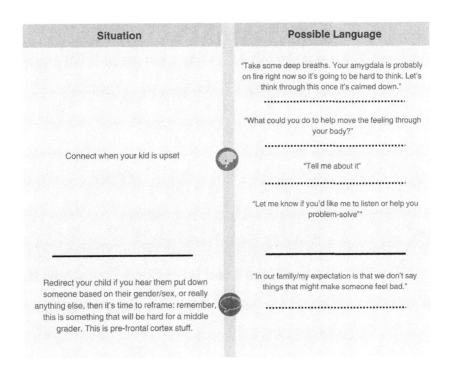

Situation	Possible Language
	"Take some deep breaths. Your amygdala is probably on fire right now so it's going to be hard to think. Let's think through this once it's calmed down."
	"What could you do to help move the feeling through your body?"
Connect when your kid is upset	"Tell me about it"
	"Let me know if you'd like me to listen or help you problem-solve"*
Redirect your child if you hear them put down someone based on their gender/sex, or really anything else, then it's time to reframe: remember, this is something that will be hard for a middle grader. This is pre-frontal cortex stuff.	"In our family/my expectation is that we don't say things that might make someone feel bad."

Situation	Possible Language
	"In our family, we judge people based on what they do and how they treat us and this doesn't sound like that."
	••
	"We respect each other's differences. Let's aim to do that next time."
	••
	"It's important to our family that we use language that recognizes and respects people's differences. Let's be more mindful of the language we use."
Set boundaries when necessary	"In our family going to school isn't optional. Let me know if you want me to take you or mom."
Advocate for themselves:	It sounds like things are getting worse with your interactions with ____. What do you think a next step could be that would help move things toward repair?
Remind them of empathy:	"In our family, we use our words to lift people up. Today your words hurt Jason. How will you help him feel better and repair the relationship?"

3

It's Time for Identity Exploration

Personal Inventory

When you were nine, what were you passionate about?
Was there a thing you were super into?
What did you like to do?
What were your hobbies?
Did you play a sport?
What about an art form (music, dance, drama, visual arts)?
What was your favorite thing to do at school?
What did you want to be when you "grew up"?

What about when you were 11?
What about when you were 12?
14?

How did things change?
When did you begin thinking about politics?
When did you realize your parents didn't (gasp) know
    everything?

Think about these things before delving into this chapter. While
a lot of the individuation process and identity formation takes
place later in high school, its seeds begin to sprout in middle
school and you can see the formation of what's to come.

DOI: 10.4324/9781003527831-4

"Everybody Rides the Carousel": Identity vs. Identity Confusion

It is a little-known, but of course, Google-able fact, that Meryl Streep's first film credit, a voice-over part, was for an animated film titled "Everybody Rides the Carousel," depicting each of the eight stages of life as theorized by psychoanalyst Erik Erikson (Hubley et al.).

Each of these eight stages deals with a human being's need to feel control over the environment as well as a need to feel a sense of agency and efficacy – to matter, to be purposeful. Each stage of life has a purpose suited to it and a goal to come out the other end integrated.

There is an infancy stage (trust vs. mistrust), early childhood (autonomy vs. shame and doubt), preschool age/play (initiative vs. guilt), school age (industry vs. inferiority), and adolescence (identity vs. identity confusion) (Orenstein). This latter stage will be the one we will concern ourselves with in this chapter. Identity formation is very important at this stage, and while no one theory will ever suit all middle graders in all places or all adolescents in all places, there are insights we can glean from Erikson's theories.

The idea that "Everybody Rides the Carousel" is an interesting one, and one I think about often. I like the idea as applied to middle schoolers – sometimes it feels like they are on *some* kind of ride. They didn't ask to get on it, they can't get off, and they are on for the duration. They are on through puberty, they are on while their brain develops, they are on while their amygdala gets hijacked, and they are on while they try to figure out who they are and who they want to be in the world. Erikson theorizes that once a middle grader hits approximately 11 or 12 that's when this exploration of different identity rules begins in earnest. This includes the exploration of goals, values, and interests (McLeod et al.).

For Erikson, the complication arises when the adolescent isn't allowed to explore these things, then they will have an "identity crisis or put on a negative identity that is more in reaction to the external world around them than in response to their own needs and purpose" (McLeod et al.).

Think about it: you're a middle grader and you're on this life carousel and you can't get off. You've got options in front of you. So many options. There are so many they are overwhelming. As we discussed in Chapter 2, a middle grader can't decide big things, like whether they are going to switch carousels or horses, or (not sure if I can keep carrying this metaphor) something like that. But they can choose what color they want their horse to be, eventually anyway, what they want to wear, and what kind of hobbies they will keep up with while they go around and around and around. What they plan to do when they grow up and what job they'll have in this carousel economy. What skills they'd like to spend more time on, or less time on. But if you're a middle grader and the grown-ups around either give you too much leeway to choose or they don't let you explore what you are good at or your identity, you'll feel either overwhelmed and frozen or stuck and trapped. And you'll *still* be going around and around. Everybody rides the carousel.

Interests and Passions

It's kind of magical if you think about all of this happening at the same time. At the end of it, should almost all of it go as well as it can go – which means a lot of mistakes, conflicts, resolutions, trials, errors, missteps, goals achieved, lots of tears, hugs, challenges, homework, math problems, soccer goals, performances, ink spilled, hangouts, text messages, triumphs, identities tried on, identities discarded – their bodies have changed and their brains have gone through a chunk of development and they know who they are and what they stand for, at least a little bit, enough to stand up for themselves and others.

It's pretty impressive. And something to celebrate.

There are few things as exciting as watching a middle grader discover a passion they have. Everyone remembers that little kids get super into dinosaurs or trains or space, but forget that middle graders can get that same intense interest, too.

One of my seventh graders this year discovered gardening. It came up, organically (no pun intended), when they were doing a lesson in STEM class, and he started caring for a bean plant.

Soon that bean plant turned into more plants and the windowsill of the STEM room wasn't enough to hold his collection.

He went to a garden store on his own time to get some additional supplies and cordoned off a section of the community garden on campus, creating a seventh-grade space that he and his friends diligently take care of now. No adult asked them to do this. In fact, it's one of those things that if an adult were more involved in, it might lose its magic for them.

Part of the joy of exploring interests at this age is the independence of that exploration.

For students who are on dance teams or play club soccer – or who do theater, or who play basketball, the middle graders are when, if the layout of the neighborhood allows, students can get to their practices or rehearsals on their own more often. Sometimes they will go out of town with their teammates, which is usually a privilege reserved for older kids.

These trips, meets, games, performances, shows, and scrimmages foster that sense of independence and help them to get a feeling of what it's like to do something seriously, to commit.

As they go through middle school, students will really start to hone in on what they think they are good at. They might start identifying themselves as a "tech person" a "sports person," a "theater person," or a "math person." Their grown-ups can help by validating their love and talent in the areas in which they feel confident – while reframing their understanding of themselves to encapsulate more of their qualities, skills, and interests and leaving things open should they change their mind about what interests them in the future.

Personal Inventory Half-Time Refresher

Remember how it felt to get your first costume?
Your first jersey from the first team you joined?
When you went to your first away meet for school?
When you got your first instrument?

Did you feel something?
Was it pride?
Did you feel grown up?
Something else?

Those feelings are the feelings of purpose and accomplishment, those feelings of being grown-up, of taking on an identity, trying it on, seeing how it feels, deciding whether it's something to keep, wear for a bit – the identity formation piece that Erikson was talking about.

Comfort Zone? Safe Zone? Or Zone of Proximal Development?

Everyone has a comfort zone. We all know what that is. We may have a literal comfort zone. Mine is my bed. Or my chair in the living room. But our figurative comfort zone, as we all know is where we feel like it's not much of a lift for us to do things, to complete a task, or to master a skill.

It's our safe zone. And there is nothing wrong with feeling safe, or comfortable!

I feel we've been told as parents that we are doing something wrong if our child is sad, uncomfortable, or anything other than content and happy. But it is in the area of (manageable) discomfort that real growth can occur. And, while being content is great, we don't *always* want our kids to be content, nor will they be. We want them to grow and expect to grow and then learn from that growth.

Lev Vygotsky, an educational theorist posited the idea of the Zone of Proximal Development, a concept well-known amongst educators. This theory takes the idea that there is a "zone of proximal development" that is between the current level of the student and the *potential* level of the student. With instruction and support, the completion of problem-solving tasks, and engagement with peers, a student would be able to reach the learning goal by working outside their current level but working in their ZPD – a sweet spot for achievement. Enough work inside the ZPD and their current level would morph into the new learning goal. Which would be the new level, and so on. Learning! (Kurt).

> The zone of proximal development consists of two important components: the student's potential development and the role of interaction with others.
>
> (Kurt)

The Zone of Proximal Development is such an important concept to understand because it goes hand in hand with a concept like a growth mindset. Too often, students try something and if they aren't good at it the first time, they don't keep trying. We want to not only help our kids develop a sense of perseverance but also show them that they can do hard things and work through struggles. Sharing with your middle grader about the idea of ZPD is a way of making their learning processes visible for them. Which can help them to continue when they may have wanted to give up. You can say, "It's normal to feel a little uncomfortable when you're out of your comfort zone, but let's look at these instructions and follow the steps and I am sure we can figure it out together." Or, "Let's take a minute, give our amygdala a chance to chill out, and remind ourselves that the learning happens in the sweet spot and that's NOT in the comfort zone."

And for a time when they're getting a sense of who they are and getting a taste of the world – well, you wouldn't want them to foreclose on options that might have been a good fit, but they didn't try because they didn't make it out of the safe zone. This isn't about forcing them to do something if they are scared, or don't want to. That is counterproductive to the purpose of helping them develop their own strong identity. In fact, if a child is being asked to do work far outside the range of their ZPD, it can make them feel inadequate. But to be in the ZPD is to allow them that beautiful feeling of self-efficacy, that feeling of "I did it!" when they've accomplished something challenging that was, indeed, a challenge for them. There's no feeling like it. How will you know if things are too comfortable, in the ZPD range, or too far out of the ZPD? Have a conversation: share about ZPD and ask them to approximate where they are.

Extracurriculars and the Renaissance Child

Of course, not all kids are the same. In fact, In my own house, I've got two opposites in terms of extracurriculars.

Child #1 loves computers, and spends all his time coding and making games. He enjoys seeing his friends, but overall an introvert. Used to take violin/piano, but despite aptitude, he didn't enjoy it. He is great at art, but doesn't always pursue it.

Child #2 wants to be with friends all. The. Time. Had to pare down his extracurriculars to only three at a time. He settled on theater, piano, and school sports.

I use my kids as examples not because either is in a better situation than the other. Both are good people. One wants to work at Google, the other wants to be an actor. We'll see what happens.

When I was their age, I wanted to be an actor too. Their dad wanted to be a writer. No one knows how the world will turn out.

Both kids have their strengths and challenges. However, when talking about students exploring their passions, forming their identities, and allowing them to explore, a kid's temperament must also be taken into consideration. You might have a kid who needs to be pushed out of their comfort zone, as was discussed in the last section, or you might have a kid who needs to be pulled back a bit to breathe and reflect on what they are doing.

For everything related to extracurriculars, it's got to be a balance. That is what I've needed to do for both my kids who tend toward extreme ends – move them toward the middle. Extracurriculars can bring out intensity, somehow. When you're in them, and in that zone, it can seem like that is all that exists. Here are some tips for balancing intensity and calm, and some of the advantages of extracurriculars:

♦ There is time for intensity later, there has to be a balance of fun and commitment.

◆ They can be a great place to learn how to keep commitments and learn discipline. So make sure you DO keep your commitments.

◆ Consider the family's schedule before committing: If it's too much of a commitment, figure it out early on and say "No. We can't do this, it's too much for our family." Have conversations before commitments are made so that everyone involved knows what the requirements are going to look like. Often, unless a family has money to burn somehow, everyone has to sacrifice time or money, and often, especially if there is more than one child, many schedules need to be balanced.

◆ They are a great way to build community and make friendships in or outside of school.

◆ They can be, depending on what the extracurricular is, a great place to learn teamwork.

◆ A growth mindset can be applied in sports or the arts, too. For some reason, students swallow feedback in this context even more than in academic contexts.

◆ If your kid's extracurricular is a big time commitment, make sure they are aware of the tradeoffs and that it is worth it to them.

◆ If your student needs to excel in an extracurricular to get into a particular high school or for another reason, make sure to view the proper psychological support. That is a lot of pressure on a kid.

◆ Purpose and mastery can be fun in itself. (Erikson would super agree with this.)

◆ Instructors should be focused on improvement and goal-setting. If your kid leaves practice demoralized on the regular, that is an issue and they will need you to step in (grown-up time). A bad day here and there is expected, but having a bad time daily isn't worth it, nor is it normal, for an extracurricular.

◆ Extracurriculars, music, dance, art, and sports are important to have a well-rounded experience of life! You want your kids to be renaissance kids.

♦ Money is a thing: Try a buy-nothing site for free gear. These sports can be expensive and kids grow quickly. You can also have a swap for hand-me-downs at the studio where your kids dance, or at the field where your kids play. It's worth a shot.

♦ Kids are multifaceted let them explore different things at this age, they don't have to be good at everything. See what they have an affinity for, and what they like to do.

♦ If your kid tells you they want to quit piano, sports, soccer, swimming, or whatever it is they're taking right before the thing, it's most likely because they are tired or want to hang out. Don't engage. **Do not have a conversation about the activity right before the activity.** Family rule. If they really mean it, they will bring it up later.

I am so serious about this last rule. I can't tell you how many times my kids have tried to pull this.

So many.

For something as important to creating a whole child as extracurriculars are – the arts, sports, and opportunities for independence and exploration in different areas – there is a massive equity gap in terms of who has access to extracurriculars and the type and quality of extracurriculars that students have access to. Many of these extracurriculars require not only an extensive parental/grown-up time commitment on weeknights and weekends that may not be possible but also often require a prohibitive amount of money to participate. These barriers not only prevent students from enjoying all of the community aspects that extracurriculars can offer but also the opportunity gap to pursue interests and passions – to explore identity and potential in the way that they should be able to (Fisher and Anderson). Extracurriculars are a way for students to round out their educational experiences, taking their interests and exploring others, and should be available to ALL students. Fischer and Anderson, in their article in *EdSurge News*, discuss programs, such as Outschool, that mitigate to a certain extent, some of these issues, some of which came to the fore even more during the pandemic (the article was written in 2019). Online programs like Outschool have minimal overheads and don't require transportation so don't cost as much as normal extracurriculars. They can be more affordable and are a possible option for families. However, they say, the systems that create the inequities and the opportunity gaps need to be further addressed. Hear, hear.

Generation Gaps: When New Ideas and Family Clash

There's nothing certain middle-grade kids like more than to poke the bear.

What bear? Any bear. They just like poking bears. They've got their little middle-grade hands out and they're ready for bear poking.

Not all middle-grade kids, but some will argue with you a lot. Now that they've reached formal operations and they've learned a bit of history and they have a slight feeling of irritation that you didn't tell them the WHOLE STORY of things when they were like, five, they are going to take it out on you now. And they think they've figured it all out.

Personal Inventory
Remember when *you* thought you had it figured out? Remember when you thought you knew *everything*?

That's how they feel now. It's awesome. And hilarious. And exhausting.

They might start talking about their feelings about politics, God, government, society, and ethics – these are all kinds of new realms of thought for them, and their views – while presented as fixed – are their first forays into this kind of discourse. Some of the views they have right now might upset you – they might be – subconsciously or intentionally – provocative or the antithesis of your ideas. Thinking differently about things is their way of individuating. Part of this process, in addition to moving from family to outside activities, from family to friends, is developing their lens on the world.

They also might start expressing dislike for things they used to like. They might start looking down on what you like. This, while it can be irritating, is the way they figure out that *they* like what *they* like – and not like something just because it's what they've grown up doing.

And when they are doing all this, it is vital to remind them that there are expectations of how to disagree with people in civil ways – and that everyone – parents, teachers, classmates – needs to be treated with dignity, regardless.

They'll roll their eyes, and say something like "Sure, whatever." But they will remember the expectation.

A Word about Hopes and Dreams

When your child is born, there is a natural feeling to project your wishes, not necessarily specific wishes – an amalgam of every wish you ever had perhaps, all the wishes in the world, everything that ever was, onto that child at this one point in their life.

This is especially easy when they are a baby. They can't talk, it's not fully clear who they are yet, though, as we, grown-ups of middle graders know, those of us who were there, could kind of tell character from the beginning.

This is normal and human. This is why we have fairy tales.

I've imagined my children in all kinds of tales in my brain that are specific to the daydreams and machinations of my imagination and projections. Ideas that I've seen in them that spark something I've thought of that interests ME, a depth I've seen in them that has resonated with themes that I've examined in my own mind, and…

All of this to say:

I say this thing a lot. I say it with a sense of pride, a sense of awe, a sense of relief, a sense of resignation, of exhaustion, of confusion:

You get the kid you get.

You get the kid you get.

(And, they'd tell you in any kindergarten worth its salt: you don't get upset.)

It's true though. You don't get upset.

Those dreams you had were never about your kid. They were projections of your soul onto your child, gifts to them that they choose to take or discard, they are by no means under any obligation to keep the gifts of your interests that you've bestowed on them.

You can focus on the interests they've rejected, or you can focus on the things they keep.

Some of them are superficial, but for a middle grader, those can often be very important, like whether you both like cheese or the same kind of music.

Some are much more important to us, like our values.

And some are about temperament. Maybe, you can appreciate, like I can, the way that my oldest child can just be in a room, silently – calmly.

Some are really about who they will become and whether they will be successful.

Again, these are OUR hopes and dreams.

This is the time when these hopes and dreams of who we thought our kid was, maybe a scholar, an athlete, or a musician, collide with who they are or who they want to be. This is why this time of individuation is hard. It's a chasm between our hopes and dreams, their idea of themselves, our idea of them, and whatever was built in between.

They are who they are. We make a mistake when we assume deficit thinking. Our dreams are no better than who they are or what their reality is and is going to be. It just means we are only working inside the confines of our own imagination. If we can push out a bit, we can support them better and will be able to appreciate their gifts so much more.

Talk Middle Grader to Me: Chapter 3

Situation	Possible Language
Your kid says they want to quit an activity right before the activity	DO NOT ENGAGE. They are tired! They want to chill. Of course, they don't want to chill! Given the option, sometimes everyone needs a push to do a thing. No quitting right before a thing."I won't have this conversation with you before _____. It is an important conversation and I want to give it the time it deserves."

| Your middle grader is uncomfortable getting out of their comfort zone, trying something for the first time | "It's normal to feel a little uncomfortable when you're out of your comfort zone, but let's look at these instructions and follow the steps and I am sure we can figure it out together."

"Let's take a minute, give our amygdala a chance to chill out, and remind ourselves that the learning happens in the sweet spot and that's NOT in the comfort zone." |

Situation	Possible Language
Your middle grader has expressed an idea in a less than polite way/disagrees with you in a way that doesn't treat you/someone else with dignity	"Even when we disagree, we speak to each other with dignity. You don't have to agree with me, and I don't have to agree with you, and we can explain our reasoning on the merits of our ideas - not by attacking each other's character." •• "We respect each other's differences. Let's aim to do that next time." •• "It's important to our family that we use language that recognizes and respects people's differences. Let's be more mindful of the language we use."

4

The Changing Social Dynamics of Middle School

Personal Inventory

When did you start wanting to hang out with friends more than being with family?

Did you?

Did you have one friend group or did you try different groups out?

Did you feel excluded?

Were you lonely a lot?

Did you hang out with a couple of close friends? Friends from school or outside of school?

Were your friends mean to you?

Nice to you?

Were you nice to your friends?

What did you do together?

Did you have romantic relationships?

How did your relationship with your parents/grown-ups shift when you began focusing on friends more?

DOI: 10.4324/9781003527831-5

If you think back, and you can remember how you felt and what you liked and how you were, you'll remember a distinct shift – perhaps even an ick feeling at times happening all of a sudden – toward your parents that you hadn't felt before. Suddenly your family weren't the people you wanted to run to in the same way you did before – instead, you looked to your friends.

The good news, dear reader, is that middle graders are, you guessed it, in the middle of this transition, and, of course, no adolescence experience is the same. So you don't need to expect a full push out just yet, in fact, the better balance you can keep of a haven of home that provides unconditional, but not clingy, positive regard, the easier things will be for your middle grader when things go sideways with friends, which they inevitably will.

There are challenges with friends at this age because they are spending more *time* with friends, and the more time you spend with people, the more opportunity you have to get irritated. Furthermore, they are still figuring out how to relate to other people and how to be a good friend. So there are going to be some dips in their relationships. They will also hang out with people who won't be a great friend fit at first. This is how they figure out who they gel with and who they don't. The most important thing is that these dips in their social life and friendships are expected, contextualized, and worked through. They are not the end of the world. They are the template for conflict resolution for life. So if you want a kid who will grow into an adult who can calmly, directly, and respectfully work through issues with others, this is where the ground is going to be laid for that kind of skill and habit (says the author who is still working on this particular skill that she definitely didn't learn in middle school).

The Importance of Friendships in the Middle Grades: Student Identity and Sense of Self

Your friends are a mirror; they tell you who you are and who you want to be. That's why kids so badly want to be with whom they perceive to be in the popular group. In reality, there are always a few different groups and each has its mores, cache, and particular ethos.

In Chapter 3, we talked about how middle graders are exploring who they are, and what they are interested in – well, this is part of it. Part of how they figure out what they are interested in is by figuring out WHO they are interested in. Part of that is learning about the qualities they seek in a friend, what they value in another human being, and how they want to feel when they are around someone else – and, what they get up to together and enjoy doing together – what they have an affinity for.

Friendship turnover in the middle grades is expected. Kids at this age, because of the identity formation and because of the different rates that their brains and their bodies are developing, will choose those around them (proximity) who have a similar level of development as they do (this can be what they perceive as status).

Friendships at this age, are, say it with me, fluid: this can be great if the current group your middle grader runs with isn't meeting their social needs, or if they are left out of the social dynamic. But what can happen, because of the differing timelines of growth, is that best friends in elementary school both slowly and suddenly grow apart. Remember Charlotte and Lena back in Chapter 1? There's the rub. The good news is, that the friendships WILL change again.

I have said "Friendships are fluid at this age" probably more times than I have said anything else in my current role in middle school. And they ARE. Many kids in fifth and sixth grade run in packs. Some don't. And then it switches. Two or three in one pack are close for two weeks you get used to it, and then it changes again. In seventh and eighth grade, it can be more varied. There are often more twos and threes than before, but they also run in large groups too. And they will switch groups. One or more people will change their interests over the summer. There is a reason this is a trope in almost all middle school-aged books, movies, and shows. But as adults, it's hard for us to remember this fluidity and how QUICKLY it happens. And so often parents get concerned that their kid doesn't have one close friend, or that they are friendly "with everyone" but aren't sticking to anyone specific. This is all within the realm of social norms for this age. It's also risky to plan really big things based on school friendships at this age – big things like school changes. That friendship, while solid for years, could change with a new social dynamic. Often, friends outside of school tend to be more stable because they are seen in isolation and the fluidity isn't part of the equation.

To *know* it's fluid is one thing, but accepting it is another. The best thing to do is know that if things are socially challenging right now, it's going to change. And if things are great right now, don't plan the wedding...or the friend equivalent of a wedding.

Kids don't think a lot about why they want to be friends with a particular person. They just WANT it, they FEEL it. So if they seem to be pursuing a friendship that hasn't taken off, but they are still hoping for, see if you can get more information. Reflection can be helpful – at the very least in allowing your middle grader to think about how they interact with friends and how they expect to be treated by others:

What do you like about ___?
How do you think it would be if you were their friend?
How do you think they will treat you?

In my experience with middle-grade students, three main factors play into friendships at this age: proximity – possibly the most important piece, affinities, and perceived similar status/level of "coolness," which you could also say is worldliness or maturity. Firstborn kids aren't often as worldly as kids who have older siblings who have been exposed to more media.

Affinity and group norms can work hand in hand. For example, students who have strong work ethics and focus on school work will have that group norm as a primary value, which will then define the group as it goes forward. These definitions tend to be strong, though each group tends to have a few, often based on those interests and affinities.

MIDDLE SCHOOL FRIENDSHIPS

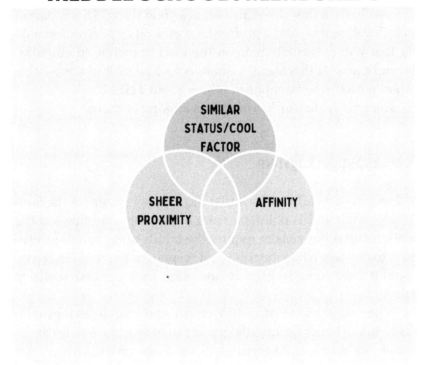

The self is important, but the self as a part of the group is often more important. This is why, when friendships break down in the middle grades, in addition to the foundational challenges of puberty and what's happening in the brain, it can be incredibly upsetting for all parties.

Is Everybody Looking at Me?

Peers taking a greater role in your middle grader's life means that they are taking a greater role in your middle grader's thoughts as well. Middle graders begin to suffer and exalt in the idea that they are unique in the world (maybe not wrong), and that others have a high-key investment in what they look like and what they do, a concept called the "imaginary audience" (definitely not right) and that their experiences and feelings are unique, special, and of merit in some way, their "personal fable" (nope!) (Anthony, "Cognitive Development").

What's good about this is that they realized that people think differently than they do – this part is a good thing. This is part of their development, and a prefrontal cortex bit of perspective-taking that will eventually help on the road to increased empathy. But right now at this stage, it often looks like a bit of a pre-occupation with the perceptions of others about THEM.

They really do think everyone is looking at them.

Peers as Support System

As I mentioned earlier, it isn't that the support system of the family goes away at this point, far from it. The ebbs and flows of the relationship roller-coaster require the family and grown-up situation to be somewhere hopefully of respite for the middle grader – so if it's not going so great in one place, they can take solace at home.

When these friendships shift, churn, and change, as they will, it is so much better for middle graders to have a place they can go to feel like they can be themselves. In terms of friendships, not all students want the draw of the hierarchical cool and popular group, that is where most of the fluidity will occur (Cornwall). Some students prefer to have their solid one or two friends they can rely on. Sometimes your middle grader WILL have that best friend, but all the more upsetting should something go awry with that friendship. It can be akin to a breakup.

According to Johnson et al., the quality of relationships in middle school accounts for 33% to 40% of the variance in academic achievement in middle school students (2010). This is a big deal and the reason why so much ink is spilled about social-emotional learning, friendships, and puberty is because they are the foundation upon which the house of academics, ethics, critical thinking, and performance is built.

Not only do friend groups support each other by just being with each other, by merely existing (just knowing that you have friends – that they are there for you – is often quite a balm for a middle-grade student in a time of challenge), but they take very active roles of support with each other in times of crisis, big and small. They are practicing how to be caretakers to each other, the way they've seen adults do for each other. It's a way that they can take on more grown-up responsibilities. One important thing to remind them of though is that they are still a kid. While they are probably doing GREAT at supporting their friend through their trouble, if it ends up being a THING, they must must must get an adult. As Damour notes, too, in her book *The Emotional Lives of Teenagers*, being there for each other, adolescents are "Tremendously supportive of one another" and can get into a place where they are "Sacrificing their own schoolwork and sleep, to talk or text with a friend who is suffering" (61).

Even if your middle grader hasn't shared with you that something is a THING, if you see that your kid is spending an inordinate amount of time playing psychologist with a particular friend, it's time to step in and help facilitate finding a *real* psychologist for their friend. Middle graders are still children, and they love to play, but it doesn't mean it's a good idea.

These support systems middle graders build, of friendships – affinity groups of one or more like-minded goofy kids with whom they want to spend their time – are not just for fun. They are the middle grader's equivalent of the pre-schooler's play. Hanging out in middle school is like imaginative playtime for two-six-year-olds. It can't be skimped on, skipped, or fast-forwarded through. And neither can the conflicts that come with it.

And that's good.

But, CONFLICT!

GOOD?

Yes. It's good. The middle grades are where they practice habits of self-advocacy, advocacy for others, and conflict resolution skills. They can learn to be direct, but respect other's dignity, and they will be OK.

I have spent a lot of time in my career as an educator resolving conflict.

Most conflict requires personal reflection at its heart. I use two protocols to guide students on conflict resolution, one interpersonal and the other intrapersonal. Some of it is done one-on-one, to get them to a place to be able to speak to the other student in a way that can honor the other's dignity or to get them to feel comfortable feeling that they can be strong enough to speak with that other student at all.

Many times when a student has made a mistake, has missed the mark, has come to be "disciplined," or, as everyone calls it, is "in trouble," the real work first needs to be internal. Sometimes the conflict resolution protocol below happens first to figure out just what HAPPENED, but often they happen in tandem, one following the other.

These processes, while I use them in a school setting, can be adapted to be used anywhere. They are based on principles of self-reflection and repairing what is broken.

Intrapersonal Steps to Conflict Resolution Protocol

It's a misnomer to call this an intrapersonal protocol, considering in order to have this kind of conflict you need another human involved, that being said, much of it is done through self-reflection.

One thing that I love about the middle grades is that mistakes are expected. And not just expected, but *necessary* for learning. In some ways, this can be why this stage feels so challenging for students, and grown-ups. There are going to be some missteps in this process – life with its changes unfolds too quickly to avoid them.

But the mistakes can be where the learning happens. Repair and conflict resolution is that learning – and this is a process that both requires and builds the skills of self-reflection, perspective-taking, and taking responsibility for the self, others, and the community. Middle graders are good humans, and good humans make mistakes. It is how they handle themselves, take responsibility, and do the hard work of repairing *after* those mistakes that challenges them to show who they are on the inside.

So whether they need the intrapersonal work first, concurrently with the interpersonal conflict resolution work, whether the repair piece took an hour, a few minutes, or several days, doing this kind of work for conflict will help them to be better humans.

It can be very challenging for middle graders to take responsibility. Some kids need time before they can even get to that step. They need to get to the place where their amygdala can step down from its stance of wanting to break everything in its path. Wait for that. Your middle grader won't be able to do the work until they get there.

Make sure, at this stage, at least to the early middle grader, that you monitor the apology. Don't write it for them, but you don't want something like: "I'm sorry you think I did something wrong," or "I am sorry you were upset," or the middle-grade classic: "I was just kidding." You want the apology to be direct and honest. The best part is your middle grader already has a template – use the protocol:

Dear _____,
I am sorry I _____. I take full responsibility for _____. I shouldn't have_____. I owe you a full apology. I intend to make it up to you by _____. You deserve to be treated with dignity. I won't make this mistake again. I will be working on making sure that I don't ___ again.
Your friend,

_____

The repair should be as related as possible to the offense. If they say something mean, they can say something kind. If they break something, they can fix it. The idea is to show that they are committed to repairing the relationship.

And that is the key to conflict resolution. When we ignore conflict or sweep it under the rug, we miss opportunities to let the light in, and the breaks just keep getting bigger and bigger.

INTRAPERSONAL STEPS TO CONFLICT RESOLUTION PROTOCOL

STEP 1: REFLECT AND TAKE RESPONSIBILITY

STEP 2: APOLOGIZE TO THE PERSON(S) AFFECTED

STEP 3: IDENTIFY AND TAKE ACTION TO MAKE NECESSARY REPAIRS TO THE SITUATION/RELATIONSHIP

STEP 4: IF IN THE SAME SITUATION AGAIN, DO NOT MAKE THE SAME MISTAKE.

Interpersonal Conflict Resolution Protocol

So much of life experience relies on perspective, and so much of perspective is subjective.

As we saw in Chapter 2, the prefrontal cortex, which helps with things like empathy and taking other people's perspectives, is not yet developed in middle graders. So it stands to reason that, when emotions are heightened, the amygdala's raring to go, and there is no way that anyone else's experience is going to make a dent in the subjective experience of a middle grader.

My job is often to get to the bottom of situations, which is always interesting, considering all of the above. What I find helpful is asking students to tell me just what happened. It's still obviously, their subjective experience, and there are always discrepancies, but I can better get a read on what happened if I stop them and say, "No, not why do you *think* she said that, what words did she *say*."

I find it also helps them, just telling me with no evaluation or inference, to discern what was a possibly unnecessary response – while they are retelling the story to me. For example, "I thought she was saying such-and-such, but maybe I misunderstood." I'll make a note of it, and then ask them to continue sharing.

After I have spoken to one student, I do the same for the other, then speak to anyone else relevant to the situation. Asking, again, not for opinions, inferences, or evaluation (as best as possible, knowing an unbiased witness statement is an impossibility). Then, we talk it out. We've got the details, and we discuss what happened. Truth is important to them, but feelings are also important. So those "I" statements are key.

Whenever students are speaking to each other in conflict resolution or I am mediating between students, there are three rules:

1. The person who has the talking piece is the one who speaks.
2. "I statements" only.
3. Give each other the benefit of the doubt.

Middle graders have a lot of trouble with the talking piece, especially when they are sharing about how they perceive things went down. But every time they interrupt each other, it's my job as the facilitator to stop them and remind them of the rule. They must learn that their words matter. That they have space to share them. It's very powerful to have space to share your words. A talking piece, which can be anything (I have a stuffed heart that I use) is a physical and tangible reminder of that space. I find that to not compound taking the space from the student talking, I will make a physical gesture, usually a stop motion with my hand, and point to the talking piece – as a reminder that this is their time. It's important, of course, to make it clear at the beginning that everyone will get a chance to speak. And they can now feel empowered to explain why they made the choices they made: "When you said such-and-such, I thought ___ and I ____." Then, they respond to each other's share, explaining their perspectives, and finally, saying what they need to move forward. They don't *want* to be in conflict.

Part of what works about this type of conflict resolution is the amount of time it takes and the fact that it is protocol-based. Both parties are heard by both a grown-up and each other, and by this point, they've usually apologized to each other organically. This can be a weight off.

It's treating each other with dignity, speaking for themselves, and holding space for the other that allows for the resolution of conflict without adding *additional* conflict.

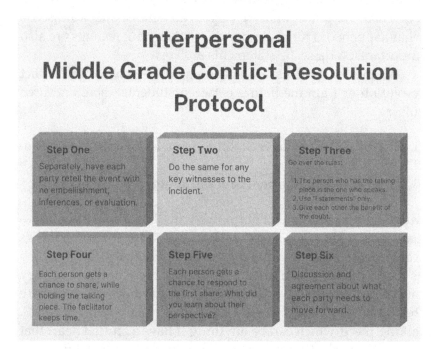

Interpersonal Middle Grade Conflict Resolution Protocol

Step One
Separately, have each party retell the event with no embellishment, inferences, or evaluation.

Step Two
Do the same for any key witnesses to the incident.

Step Three
Go over the rules:
1. The person who has the talking piece is the one who speaks.
2. Use "I statements" only.
3. Give each other the benefit of the doubt.

Step Four
Each person gets a chance to share, while holding the talking piece. The facilitator keeps time.

Step Five
Each person gets a chance to respond to the first share: What did you learn about their perspective?

Step Six
Discussion and agreement about what each party needs to move forward.

The Partnership between School and Home

Conflict is a part of life, and indeed, a part of middle school. Most classes employ pedagogical strategies and projects that require teamwork, which requires collaboration. This can be a challenge if your goal is to avoid conflict or avoid conflict for your kid because any teacher will tell you that in a group work period, there are more small to medium conflicts in a group project than can be counted on two hands. When managed skillfully, these conflicts are mitigated and resolved so that each group member feels seen and heard and so that each person feels like they have had a chance to share their perspective. The thing I most often hear as the biggest issue is "They weren't listening to my ideas." People want to be heard. It makes people feel less than if they aren't.

Feeling like no one listens to you or like you can't get a word in edgewise or like you are always spoken over is one way that kids exert control over each other. But there are other ways in which kids jockey for control. There is conflict in the middle grades that spills over into unkindness, and sometimes more than unkindness. For those instances, research shows that it's hard for students at risk of being the target of that kind of behavior to demonstrate cognitive effort in the classroom, to engage, and to develop positive feelings toward school (Bélanger, 2023). The school, families/grown-ups, and students must work together to eradicate situations like this once when they occur to avoid negative outcomes. Because in the middle grades especially, it is something everyone needs to work on together.

Middle graders are still children – the oldest among them being 14, there has to be a partnership between the school and families. The ideal is for the school to be the place where many of the social interactions take place with the concentration of educators schooled in social-emotional learning and interventions for these kinds of behaviors. And at home, families/grown-ups have a strong hold on the value systems of the children, what they believe in, and the boundaries that will be enforced for them – together, this can be a strong system to keep students from going too far off course.

Speaking Up in a Group

Some groups are more inclusive than others. Some of this depends on the personalities that are dominating the groups. If they are inclusive, eternally kind, and supportive, the ethos of the group will be more aligned with those values.

But don't be fooled. Each kid in a group has agency because each one of these kids is going through all this. So no one feels completely confident, in touch with themself and who they are, and is fully OK with what they do. So if someone in the group feels like something is amiss and calls out someone on their behavior, it can have quite an effect.

This is a powerful way of combating unkindness. It's hard for kids to do, but it's important for middle graders to feel like it's a tool in their toolbox. A tool that they can use to someone, even if they perceive that someone has more social power than they have to "stop" or "that crossed a line."

I experienced this recently in a middle-grade chat group.

The circumstances were as similar as they are to most any other time a middle grader violates boundaries of what is appropriate to say – whether mean, sexual, violent, or otherwise. The circumstances of this particular incident are only incidental to this example. But instead of pretending it didn't happen, continuing the chat, or everyone going along with the conversation, one child wrote back, "This crossed a line. You shouldn't have said it."

Another child followed suit. Writing a similar thing.

After a while, apologies followed.

If that sounds like a best-case scenario. It is. It won't always end that well. But it is an example of it being effective – in all ways – to cause the person who stepped over the line to rethink and to empower the group to reflect.

How to Talk to Your Middle Grader: Kids Can Be Mean in Middle School

Kids are trying new things out at this age and sometimes that affects how they treat others.

It's important to ask your kid if they bring you a situation: Would you like me to listen or are you looking to problem-solve?

Going back to the Personal Inventory and why we take it at the beginning of each chapter – sometimes we can overreact to a situation that is uncomfortable for our kids but is just part of the growing process. Make sure to listen, not react.

And you go from there.

Help your kid contextualize what happened and ask what they need to be able to move forward.

Make sure your kid knows that they deserve dignity. How will you let them know? You'll tell them. A lot. They'll love that. Middle graders LOVE IT when you tell them stuff like that. I'm kidding, they'll hate it, but at some point, they'll believe it. Because it's true. They deserve dignity, just like everyone else.

Make sure your kid has an adult they can go to at school. Because if most of this stuff is going on at school, you're going to want someone at school to handle should it need to be ramped up and handled by a grown-up. You're not at school, so guide your middle grader to approach a teacher or another grown-up they can talk to if they need to escalate it.

Give space, and time, and make sure that your response isn't extreme, you want your kid to come to you in the future. If you make a thing of it they won't come next time because they will worry you will "react." The key is, even if it's a THING (remember, a THING?) you don't have to crazy react. You just have to ACT. The reaction is what bugs them. It makes them uncomfortable because *everything* you do makes them uncomfortable. Because you are their grown-up. They don't like how you sit, how you talk, or how you walk through a room.

One of my kids told me the other day that I "vacuum weird." So, yeah. Don't react.

And make sure to follow up. In a few days, offhandedly ask "How is that thing going?" They will let you know if it's still a thing. The best-case scenario is they don't know what you're talking about and you have to clarify.

Most middle-grade issues are resolved organically

If your student's issue does not, it may be that you need to discuss it with your student's teacher or advisor or another person in their school.

Because they *will* have interpersonal issues. It could be over a group project, a friend who is distancing themselves, or they may feel like they are being targeted in some way. Some issues are high-level, and those need to be dealt with seriously. But most middle-grade conflicts are not at that level. If it's at that level, then it's at least a THING. Then it likely needs to involve multiple sets of grown-ups, school personnel, and depending on what it is, a school counselor or outside practitioner.

Now, If you find out your kid is the one *being* mean. It's important to get all the info and context. Things like this are almost always complicated and rarely straightforward. As a parent you might feel ashamed or, conversely, you might feel like your kids' actions are justified by the context.

But don't let your feelings get in the way of the learning process for your kid.

Focus on the actions and the words that your students used.

Discuss alternatives. What could they have done differently? Could they have said nothing? Could they have walked away? Usually, those two things are often the best choices.

Believe it or not, many kids don't actually realize they are being mean. You have to show them, and in a way that they will see it.

Your student needs to hear: "I have high expectations for how you treat people because this is value important to our family and I know you can meet these expectations."

"So how will you go about repairing this? And what is the plan next time you are in a similar situation? Because what happened this time isn't an option. Let's brainstorm together."

The feelings that come up when YOUR kid has been mean can overshadow all logic. Don't let them explain away their behavior, hold the line. No matter what, you can have high expectations for how they treat others. And if they slip up, you can help them repair it. No dignity was lost for them, but a lesson well learned.

Listen to your kid about their experience and feelings. Reassure them that their value, worth, and dignity are not predicated on anyone else's approval. Help them to see that if someone is mean to them, it isn't necessarily because of THEM, but is more a reflection of the person who is being mean. Validate the feelings and remind them that they are strong and that there is a larger context to see. This experience will equip them with another layer of emotional fortitude they can rely upon the next time they are in a situation like this – another social-emotional tool in their toolbelt.

Sometimes a tool just looks like making it through a challenging experience.

Dignity vs. Respect

Rosalind Wiseman, author of *Queen Bees and Wannabees*, the book *Mean Girls* was based on, speaks about creating cultures of dignity in her work. She makes the distinction, and this is an important distinction, and one that is key for this age group, between respect and dignity.

Dignity is the idea that everyone has inherent value. And not only that everyone has it, but that everyone's inherent value is the same. It's immutable, non-transferable, unbreakable, and non-negotiable. She says in her book *Owning Up*, "While we are all born with dignity, we are not born knowing how to act in ways that honor everyone's dignity...these skills must be practiced" (1).

The concept of dignity vs. respect is something that can be practiced and Wiseman has a curriculum for use in schools. But beyond schools, treating others with dignity can be modeled by a middle grader's grown-ups and discussed reflectively to make an impact, adding to the ethical toolbox of how to treat others.

For students, this differentiation between respect and dignity is very important and comes out a lot, especially in relationships with adults. Wiseman shares that when she asks young people what they think of when they think of respect, they think:

Respect is supposed to be earned, but it's usually imposed.
I have to obey them no matter how they treat me.
If they don't respect me, then I don't have to respect them.

She continues, "The definition of respect is to admire someone for their actions, traits, or accomplishments. It is earned or lost through their actions, choices, and behaviors" (2).

And truthfully, schools and often the grown-ups of middle graders have used the word respect synonymously with the concept of compliance. Respect often *means* compliance. For many teachers and parents, to respect them is to comply with their rules and instructions. Respectful kids are the quiet kids. Respectful kids are the ones who do what they are told.

But this lack of clarity creates a rift and missed opportunity. For one, compliance, while helpful for, say, giving safety instructions, or perhaps, instructions in general, is not actually what respect means, and students are missing the point. And so we can't be shocked when there is confusion about what respect looks like.

Wiseman argues that by using the word dignity to describe what we mean when we say "respect" we separate actions from worth. This way, you don't actually have to respect what someone does, but you cannot deny that they are worthy of being treated with dignity. They are a human being (2).

Besides getting a great deal more clarity in terms of what we expect from our students in terms of how they treat people (not just compliance but dignity, which encompasses listening, respecting boundaries, acknowledging the feelings and experiences of others, even if you don't agree with them, using inclusive language, avoiding hurtful language, giving support in times of crisis, valuing others' autonomy, and showing empathy and compassion), we also bridge a divide between middle grader and grown-up. Because if you are struggling to get along with your middle grader (gasp! never!), you can agree to treat each other with dignity, but the respect/compliance piece muddies those waters a great deal.

Maintaining a connection with your middle grader during this time can make things feel less tumultuous. And the habit of you being there, asking if they need you to just listen this time or help them problem-solve, of them coming to you if, heaven forbid, there is a THING, or later when they are in high school if they are uncomfortable and need to get out of a situation, they know they *can* trust you, you won't overreact or underreact, and you'll *be* there, treating them with dignity.

WHAT DOES IT LOOK LIKE TO TREAT SOMEONE WITH DIGNITY?

▶ ACTIVE LISTENING

▶ RESPECTING PHYSICAL AND EMOTIONAL BOUNDARIES

▶ USING INCLUSIVE LANGUAGE, AVOIDING HURTFUL LANGUAGE

▶ GIVING SUPPORT IN CRISIS

▶ VALUING AUTONOMY

▶ SHOWING EMPATHY AND COMPASSION

Talk Middle Grader to Me: Chapter 4

Situation	Possible Language
All the time	"You deserve dignity!"
Your middle-grader is sharing about something mean that happened between themself and a peer.	"Would you like me to just listen or to help you problem solve?"*
Your middle-grader was mean to a peer.	"I have high expectations for how you treat people because this is a value important to our family and I know you can meet these expectations." "So how will you go about repairing this? And what is the plan next time you are in a similar situation? Because what happened this time isn't an option. Let's brainstorm together."
During conflict resolution, getting back to the facts, as best as they can:	"No, not why do you *think* she said that, what words did she *say*."

5

The Roles of Grown-Ups in the Middle Grades

Personal Inventory

This one is about YOUR grown-ups:

What were they like?
Did you think they were too involved?
Not involved enough?

Did they prepare you for life?

On a scale of 1–10, 1 being never and 10 being all the time, how often do you think they thought about how well they were parenting you?
1   2   3   4   5   6   7   8   9   10

Conversely, on that same scale, how often do YOU think about how well you're parenting?
1   2   3   4   5   6   7   8   9   10

What was the numerical difference?

If the difference was greater than 4, why do you think that is?

What was your grown-ups' parenting style?

DOI: 10.4324/9781003527831-6

Middle School, Revisited

You're probably thinking, hey! I thought we were done with this chapter's Personal Inventory!

Sorry, but it's important. Sometimes, we need to look into the mirror and go deep:

What does it look like to accept your own middle-grade self so that you can better be there for your middle grader?

This is me and my husband in eighth grade. Both of us modeling in vogue glasses, dorky backward hats, and also proving my tri-part theory about proximity (preschool, middle school, high school, cool-ness level – both *highly* un-cool – and affinities: Stephen King, band, other stuff, Street Fighter II).

I keep this picture of my eighth-grade self in my office in a middle school to remind myself of that person *I* was in middle school. Because I was very self-conscious. I was worried about being liked. I was worried about being competent enough at my schoolwork. I was worried about my friends. I was worried about whether my boyfriend liked me. Thought incessantly about my hair, my clothes, and my skin. I wish I could have that time back. I wish I could go back and tell myself that *none* of us had it figured out.

Because it may look like some of them do, but at the end of the day, they are all middle graders. They are all kids. If it was easier for you then, that's wonderful. I had a middle grader come up to me recently and tell me like they were telling me a secret, that they think it a "good idea" if a middle schooler "rebels a little," because otherwise, they'll do it later when it's not such a good idea. I nodded, and I said, "That might be, you come back and tell me later, OK?"

Why Is It So Hard Being a Parent?

At the time I am writing this, I have been a parent for 14 years. And, while I haven't been a parent at any other time in history or anything, it seems to me that being a parent now is more challenging than before.

Surely, it *shouldn't* be harder to be a parent for several reasons:

Running water, cars, plumbing, diapers, the snot sucker, those removable car seat things, phone calendars that sync with other family members' calendars, family group texts, GPS, podcasts, double strollers, loveys, etc.

But that isn't how things have shaken out. As I alluded to in the intro, we have been inundated, like a fire hose, with so much information about child-rearing that our amygdalas are exhausted from fighting and our bodies are pumped with so much parenting cortisol that we don't know what to do with ourselves.

What I am trying to say is that it *feels* like parenting right now is stressful.

Stressful because of a conflation of a few things:

1. **Fire Hose:** Competing information on the Internet about how to do things that regularly contradict each other
2. **ALL Prevention, ALL the Time:** This idea that if something happens it was both preventable *and* our fault – so we need to DO things to make sure that things *don't* happen

3. **Total Success Principle:** Every possible thing, depending on your personal value system (academics, material wealth, network, social status, etc.) should be provided for children, and if you have it and it's *not* provided you are doing your children a disservice. If you *don't* have it, you should try to acquire it

4. **Tummy Time for All Ages:** Interaction and connection are required at almost all times to make sure your kid is OK. When they are younger this is so this is for brain development. When they are older, this is to keep them off screens and to make sure they are mentally OK.

This is a lot to try to do in a world in which we have a huge wealth disparity and the pay gap, a mindbogglingly timed school day, not at all convenient for working hours, expensive day-care and after-school and before-school care, expensive extracurriculars, cities and suburbs with less than adequate public transportation for students to take independently, especially younger than 11, a lack of extended family as a support system, and households with its grown-up(s) working. Not to mention that each of us is (probably) a human person with our own problems, jobs, relationships, needs, and stuff, and should have some time for that, too.

All of that is…a lot.

If you Google, "What is the experience of parenting now?," not "Is the experience of parenting more difficult now?" or something biased like that, the results that come up are heavily weighted toward challenge.

Studies from the University of Irvine as well as the Collegia of Carlo Alberto in Turin, Italy, showed that parents, on the whole, are spending twice as much time as they did in the 1960s on childcare. The studies attribute this to the trend of "intensive parenting." As Rebecca Holman, a journalist, writes in a Grazia article, "In short – we are doing more active parenting than we've ever done before, with less time to do it in." Intensive parenting is a style of parenting in which

Parents invest significant amounts of time, money and energy in raising their children. The "proper" approach in intensive parenting is defined as "child centred, expert guided, emotionally absorbing, labour intensive and financially expensive."

(Yerkes)

Intensive parenting may have some positive outcomes on children's physical health, but later in life, data suggests that the relationship between intensive parenting and depression levels and college students' loss of locus of control might be linked (Yerkes).

Indeed, the current United States Surgeon General, Dr. Vivek Murthy, recently issued a Surgeon General's Advisory on the state of parental mental health, citing a crisis in resources and support for parents and caregivers stating "This Advisory calls attention to the importance of parental stress, mental health and well-being, stressors unique to parenting, and the bidirectional relationship between parental mental health and child outcomes" (Murthy).

And so, then:

How can parents best support students during this time while balancing support, nurturing, and leaving room for students to try and fail on their own? How can parents help students when school and the world look so different from when they were growing up?

How can we parent, but not so...intensively? We can just be the grown-ups for your middle graders. If we take back a bit of the space we've been taking up, they can claim it with some of their newfound independence.

So with all of this information, whether you intensive parent, or not, whether you lighthouse parent, or whether you are another type of parent, or whether you get up every morning and put your pants on one leg at a time, if you are reading this book you know and care about a middle grader, you have to be the grown-up in some kind of way. So let's unpack this:

1. **Fire Hose:** It's exhausting to have to look up a billion different ways to have to do stuff all the time. Especially when one way is telling you one thing and another way is telling you another thing.

2. **ALL Prevention, ALL the Time:** It's not really fair to say that if we do this and this and this, we can prevent every bad thing because that's not true and feeds into our anxiety and our kids' anxiety

3. **Total Success Principle:** This one is hard, it's easy to get caught up in wanting your kid to have opportunities, and the more they have, the more options they have. Balance, my friends, balance.

4. **Tummy Time for All Ages:** Some people are introverts. Talk with your middle grader about how much/in what ways they like connecting. There isn't a particular time requirement.

The most important thing middle-grade grown-ups can do for their middle graders is to BE the grown-up for them. They are still children. They are 10–14.

That means that if they come to you with a problem, you breathe, and you help them through it.

Because the middle-grade stuff, while it can get dicey, as we will unpack in the next few sections, isn't usually as dicey as the high school stuff can be, and you WANT to have developed a foundation of trust and consistency in your reaction so that that know what they can expect when they come to you. They need to know that you will respond in a measured way. They need to know that you won't DO anything if the situation doesn't call for you to do anything, you won't hold anything against any of their friends if they need to vent about them, and that you can just BE there for them.

So what IS the best way to help middle graders through things?

Well, there isn't *one* best way, but I have found that in almost every situation, it helps to be three things:

Receptive, calm, and consistent.

That will keep them coming back to you. Remember, you are playing the long game.

As an educator, I like to have a nice three-word acronym or initialism so I can remember something easily. When talking to middle schoolers, remember RCC:

Receptive
Calm
Consistent

Receptive, Calm, Consistent.

If you're being receptive, you are nonjudgmental, if you're calm, you're listening, you're putting your own baggage and stuff to the side and not reacting, and if you're consistent, you are not going to apply some rules one day and not the other day. Children need boundaries, but consistent boundaries. They need to know that the rules are not going to change daily.

Gordon Neufeld and Maté Gabor in their book *Hold On to Your Kids*, chafe against the common understanding that middle school/high school-age children must orient toward their peers rather than their grown-ups, and believe strongly that children need their parents during this crucial time. They say:

> It takes three ingredients to make parenting work: a dependent being in need of being taken care of, an adult willing to assume responsibility, and a good working attachment from the child to the adult. The most critical of these is also the one most commonly overlooked and neglected: the child's attachment to the adult.
>
> (Neufeld and Gabor, 54)

My own experience has borne out a balanced approach between friends and family, and I think that to overlook the importance of independence and friends at this age would also be problematic.

In the middle grades, it *is* definitely the case that students need to have their grown-ups in a primary position. After all, their grown-ups – whoever they are – are still caring for them. A middle grader may (will) begin to start doing things independently, and that's very important, but they still are being cared for. And emotionally, while they may be pulling away a bit, they do still need their grown-ups to be receptive. They need their grown-ups to be consistent in their presence; middle grades continue to have an expectation for support and care. Attachment doesn't mean a specific action or quantifiable amount of time spent in conversation – it means a continued connection and a general feeling that their grown-up will be responsive to them – a feeling that they MATTER to their grown-up (APA).

So, remember: RCC, Receptive, Calm, Consistent. Apply these principles to conversations with your middle grader and it will be easier to maintain this attachment even during some of the more chaotic moments of the middle grades.

How to Talk to Your Middle Grader

So we've established the **"How"** for the grown-up in the conversation: Receptive, Calm, Consistent.

There's also the **"When."**

The middle grades are when kids may start spending more time on their own, in their room, if they have one. This is a normal and expected part of development at this age. Middle graders need their space. They will still seek out connection with you though. And so you have to be savvy about picking up on cues that your middle grader wants to connect. They may ask about your day. They may mention something off-handedly. They may come sit near you. These are their overtures for connection. Definitely be calm in your responses. Sometimes they're like skittish cats. But if you give them the space and calmly engage, they will know that you won't make a whole thing of it when they do try to connect. And if they are really wanting to be on their own, always remind them that you are there. You aren't going anywhere. You're their center. You're their caregiver. They really do need you.

Now for the rest: These mini-sections of the chapter discuss topics that might come up between you and your middle grader that might be difficult to discuss, and then it will address situations that might make a conversation more challenging. Some of the topics have been covered in earlier chapters, but have been distilled into a bite-sized format as a resource for conversations.

Topic: About Drugs/Alcohol

Big caveat: each family is different and will approach topics like this in their own way. Also, there is a wide range of developmental levels when approaching this particular topic. Start early. In this day and age, the first time the concept of drugs will come up isn't necessarily going to be on the playground. These kids have access to media that will expose them to the world, if not the concept, pretty early.

There are some middle graders for whom this talk will be completely abstract and hypothetical: they haven't thought about drugs, their friends are not thinking about drugs, their peers aren't really thinking about drugs, and it's not yet relevant. They still need the talk. The talk doesn't just happen once. It's ongoing, at different stages. There are middle graders for whom this ongoing talk is acutely relevant and, it may be true that they already know about these risks or consequences as a result of tragedy. Wherever your middle grader is, this is a topic that each family is going to have their own take on. Have a dialogue about these things at whatever level your child is ready for and can comprehend. Be open, calm, and clear: explain your boundaries around these things, but don't over-explain…they don't need DARE-esque stories about PCP-driven violence. But they do need some idea of what a drug is. Otherwise, they won't have a schema to be able to make healthy choices when the issue becomes pressing. The key to this, as with most everything at this age, is open communication. They need to know that you will get them if they are in a situation where they feel unsafe or pressured. They need to know that they can call you if they or someone close to them needs medical or emotional support with drugs or alcohol. They aren't going to be perfect, and it is very unlikely they will go through their middle school, high school, college, or beyond experiences without any conversations about, references to, or experiences with drugs and alcohol, so shielding them from the conversation isn't going to make it go away.

Discussing alcohol and alcohol abuse/binge drinking is important in this conversation as well, but they usually have an understanding of what alcohol is, unlike drugs, which are abstract. But that doesn't mean giving them the firehose of information.

Choose a time to talk when things are calm and relaxed. You can ask: "Have you learned anything about drugs in school yet?" or say "Remember we were watching __ and it mentioned drugs? We need to talk about it, and I am here to answer your questions as best I can."

Explain: Learning about drugs is a part of learning about health and safety.

Drugs are something you put in your body that will change your experience somehow. There are drugs for pain, like Tylenol or Advil, or drugs to help with diseases (use a relevant example for you). There are always risks with drugs, like the ones listed really fast at the end of those drug commercials.

And when people say "drugs," they are referring to a group of drugs that the body doesn't need. A category of drug where using comes with a large amount of risk that outweighs any benefit (not to mention legality in most cases). Explain: Some of these could make people feel good temporarily, but there are a lot of things in life that people can do that make them feel good that don't have the legal, relationship, school, health, and life consequences that drugs can have.

Avoid using intense scare tactics or hyperbolic stories. But they do need to know the risks. Especially about fentanyl as it *is* a risk – even when kids are just experimenting.

For fentanyl, I would make an exception to the scare tactic, because the truth is, well, scary. They need to know that some drugs that teens buy are pills that aren't prescribed to them, that will change how they feel. But instead of buying real Oxycontin, Percocet, or Xanax, they buy from people selling fake pills mixed with a cheap synthetic (manufactured) drug called fentanyl to make more money. Fentanyl doesn't taste, smell, or look like anything and the amount needed to overdose and kill is equivalent to two grains of sand. That's why one pill can kill (Greene Middle School). Tell them: don't take anything if you don't know what it is.

Encourage them to ask questions. If you don't know the answer, say so and find it out later. Share if appropriate.

The safer they feel in this conversation, the safer they will feel coming to you when the issue is pressing.

Talk about what peer pressure looks like – and what it *doesn't* look like.

It doesn't usually look like a bunch of kids different from you goading you to take something, it will look like people you know doing something and inviting you as well.

You can discuss how their true friends will accept their choices and that you are always available to come get them – should they need an out for any reason. You can have a code between you – so that their out doesn't need to be super obvious.

Be an example, and explain that in your family, the expectation is that drugs are used when prescribed by a doctor or for a medical or mental health need. And that the reason drugs are "bad" is because of addiction and harm. Addiction is a disease and a challenge to overcome.

The hope is that these boundaries will sit in their heart, but follow-up and open communication is necessary.

Topic: About Sex

Similar caveat to the drugs/alcohol section: this topic is sensitive and each family has their values around it. My suggestions come from my background in child development and middle graders.

Start Early

With this one, you won't likely have to broach the topic with them the first time it comes up. They will ask questions. The key is to give them the factual answer to what they actually asked, not all of the baggage about what they asked. Often, they will be fine with a clear, true, and simple answer.

If they *haven't* brought it up, bring it up and share basic facts.

Puberty and Hygiene

Use correct terms: penis, vagina, vulva, sperm, ovary. I would add that sex for many adults is not just about conception, but about intimacy and pleasure. Hopefully, they are learning about puberty in school. It's a great help to the family because it gives them factual information upon which to base conversations.

The relevance of sex coincides with their bodies changing. They will likely need help with details around this: menstruation – conversations about pads vs. tampons vs. cups, etc.

Skincare: "Here is what is available for kids your age and here's how to use it."

Deodorant: "Here's when to use it."

Laundry: "Do it. More often. Don't forget to move it along or it gets gross." If your family goes to a laundromat, make sure that your middle grader takes responsibility for their clothes.

Puberty and Feelings

Talk plainly and privately about the normalcy of self-touch and pleasure. Or, they may not be there and that is fine, too.

Leaving a book or two where they can read it on their own can be helpful. You definitely want them to avoid Google here when possible.

Consent

The great thing is that the conversation about consent is transferable in many scenarios. For example, one of my kids would try to hug and kiss the other because he knew it bugged his brother. We would emphasize consent is necessary for that kind of touch. The idea is, later, when you're talking about consent and sex, they have a schema for it. Consent is not just not saying no – it's saying yes. Model by asking your middle grader: Can I hug you?

Enthusiastic Consent

Then, when you talk about sex with your middle grader, you can talk about how important it is that when people are engaging in it **all parties want to.**

Internet Pornography

The term encapsulates a wide range of available videos and images – on a spectrum of anodyne to harmful/violent/illegal. In my experience, middle graders have *a lot* of questions about pornography. They are pretty sure it's bad, and they want to know *why* it's bad. This is where you can dovetail conversations about enthusiastic consent about those involved, what is appropriate for consenting adults, and what is never OK: violence and abuse. You can share that it's not necessarily BAD, it's just that for them it's not appropriate: 1. It is illegal, though very easy, to click "over 18" on any site. 2. Most of what is available on the Internet is too much for middle graders to process. 3. There is a real danger in normalizing situations that are beyond what consenting people will often engage in and it sets up outsized expectations for students once they *do* begin to engage in sexual activity. There *can* be a benefit in normalizing kinks or sexual feelings that already exist in the student – which can lessen feelings of shame. But this is complicated. At this age, for middle graders I would say that Internet pornography *is* too much – and you can share this with them – and if you feel it's important or necessary, provide safer options for them.

STDs and Pregnancy

They may not need the info for a while, but they should know what is available in terms of pregnancy and STD prevention. They should also, of course, know about the risks of pregnancy and STDs, but that is early in the technical part of the conversation.

Keep the lines of communication open so that they know you will help them should they need something they don't have. Your kid may not be having sexual feelings yet.

Gender and Sexuality

They may have sexual feelings toward one gender over another, or both genders, or not at all, or they just aren't sure how they feel. Reminder, sexuality and gender are different. Gender identity is how they feel about who they are on the inside, and sexuality is about who they want to hold hands with/kiss. Be open, listen. This can be complicated for them. They might not be sure at this point what they are feeling. Listen, don't ask leading questions. Being nonjudgmental in listening will help them to feel seen and accepted for who they are.

You want to make sure your middle grader knows mechanics and facts, risks, consent, and enthusiastic consent, variance in feeling, and experience your openness and support for them if they need to talk, if they feel pressured, if they are worried about something or anything associated with sex.

Tip: the chiller you can be with this while holding boundaries and expectations the better.

Topic: About a Challenging Teacher

We've all had a teacher who has challenged us, inspired us, pushed us. And we've all had that teacher who we have clashed with, whose style just didn't fit for us.

As an educator, I know how challenging teaching is and how hard teachers try to meet the needs of each of their students.

And I am a person and parent, so I also know when things feel off with a teacher. When it doesn't feel like it's working or it feels the teacher doesn't really see your kid or it feels like things are too difficult for no reason. And unless true harm is being done, all this can be a learning opportunity for your middle grader.

Our generation has been told, as parents, that if we don't step in to help when something is amiss then we are doing our child a disservice. But it hasn't always been clear to what extent that holds true. It's very easy to go too far and try to ease circumstances and situations too much.

Students at this age need to learn to advocate for themselves, and, even more, they need to learn to bend to circumstances sometimes, rather than expect circumstances to bend to them.

It's important to listen to your kid: if they are frustrated, listen. Don't dismiss the concerns, reframe the concerns. Often there will be some overgeneralization your student is doing so right-sizing the issue is important.

If they feel a teacher is always saying they are the one doing something when they feel they aren't, talk through the situation. See if they can make any small changes that will help them. For example, if a teacher catches them talking in class but, they feel, only blaming them, walk through it. Could they not engage in the conversation? Could they approach the teacher to discuss later and ask for support in some way?

If a teacher's grading style seems harsh, what a great opportunity for your student to learn that they can't always control the way people view their work. They can learn that there will be people who can push you harder than you might think you are ready for, but maybe it means you are ready for it. The permutations of issues are endless, but reframing can be helpful in each situation.

If your student can approach the teacher with curiosity about their concerns, that is the best way:

> [Teacher's Name/Title], when this happens, I feel like ___. I'd like things to be different. Can you help? Or "My intentions are ____, but it seems like the impression you are getting is different than my intentions. Can we talk about it?

The next step is to go to the teacher directly. It may feel easier to approach admin, but they will talk to the teacher regardless. And teachers appreciate direct communication. Approach with curiosity:

> [Teacher's Name/Title], I was hoping we could find a time to talk. I was wondering about ___ and your perspective on it. I know we both want __ to be successful.

At the end of the day, teachers want to support their students and grown-ups want their students supported at school. Partnership is key, between the student, teacher, and home. Reframe for your student, have a direct conversation if necessary, and sometimes, being a little uncomfortable is OK.

Topic: About Their Pain and Their Hurt

Whether it's a fight with a friend, with you, a bad report card, trouble at school, a middle school breakup, an illness, a divorce, a parent who is sick, or a loss, there will be times when your middle schooler is distraught. All of these things can reach the level of true pain at this age. Emotions are heightened and coping skills aren't secure. But they will need help and support and to get that from you they will need to know that you will listen and not judge them and that you will love them and be there for them no matter what. They are feeling everything – you can help them zoom out to remember that their feelings aren't going to last forever. That they will persevere and move through. You can just be there for them. If you are concerned that your child is thinking of harming themselves or ending their life or if they need more support that you can offer, below is a list of crisis lines they can contact. You don't have to be actively in danger of ending your life to call these hotlines.

They need to know that you aren't going to react poorly to what they share – or they will think something is wrong with them, or that they will get a lecture of some kind.

Listen, Don't Advise

It is hard to see our kids in pain. So, we want to jump in and help them fix it right away. But the sharing part is really important. Don't skimp on that part. Let them start thinking of suggestions first; it's their problem, and they may already have some ideas. They may not even want advice at this time.

Validate

Validate their feelings. They need to hear that you think their feelings are important. They also need to hear that they are important and worth something. And that you care about them, so you care about their feelings. Even if these feelings are about you.

Reflect

Help them to recognize the origin of the pain. Ask a question about how their body is feeling, about what is most uncomfortable right now. We often hold most of our negative emotions in our bodies. Remind them to breathe.

Remind Them That Emotions and Feelings Are Temporary

They will not feel this way forever. Even if the situation isn't fixed, they will move through this awful feeling and come out the other end. They have done this before and they can do it this time.

Help Them Identify Something to Do

Once you've listened, validated, talked it out, breathed together... now what? What can they do to stay in this calmer place? Some options: journal, listen to music, go for a walk, talk to a friend, watch a show, etc.

Check In, But Don't Dwell

Later, check in with them again. See how they are doing. Keep it casual. Don't press the issue. Listen if they want to talk, but if they seem to have moved through, don't dwell on it.

Get Help If Needed

If you are worried that your middle grader's pain is more than they can manage and more than you can manage, seek support. Having someone to talk to who isn't a parent is important. it can be a therapist, a counselor, or another trusted adult. Seek support for yourself if you are feeling burn out by holding someone else's emotions. Make sure you have someone you can talk to as well.

If It's Too Much

if it's an acute situation, have them contact a crisis helpline or suicide prevention line. You don't have to be actively in danger of ending your life to call these hotlines. In fact, they are very good at taking someone from an acute moment of pain to a manageable cooler level of emotion.

- **National Suicide Prevention Lifeline (USA)**
  - Hotline: 1-800-273-TALK (1-800-273-8255)
- **Crisis Text Line (USA)**
  - Text "HELLO" to 741741
- **Kids Helpline (Australia)**
  - Hotline: 1800 55 1800

♦ **Childline (UK)**
  ○ Hotline: 0800 1111
♦ **Kids Help Phone (Canada)**
  ○ Hotline: 1-800-668-6868
♦ **Lifeline (New Zealand)**
  ○ Hotline: 0800 543 354
♦ **National Domestic Violence Hotline (USA)**
  ○ Hotline: 1-800-799-SAFE (1-800-799-7233)
♦ **Trevor Project (USA)**
  ○ Hotline (for LGBTQ+ youth): 1-866-488-7386
  ○ Text "START" to 678678
♦ **Trans Lifeline (USA)**
  ○ Hotline: 877-565-8860
♦ **National Eating Disorders Association (NEDA) Helpline (USA)**
  ○ Hotline: 1-800-931-2237
  ○ Text "NEDA" to 741741

Topic: About Unkindness

Middle graders will sometimes be unkind. This is true. They are working to survive, socially. They are figuring out who they are. They are jockeying for position in the hierarchy. Comparing themselves to others can make them feel better. Makes them feel "normal." This is, what we call in the biz, developmentally appropriate behavior.

As the grown-ups of middle graders, it doesn't help to be shocked when these things happen. We can help by explaining to our kids some of the developmental reasons why unkindness ramps up in middle school (puberty, super-charged amygdala, and not a lot of prefrontal cortex action).

And we can support the entire community and all of our kids by having expectations of them – that they, themselves, be better. Each time you speak to them about how to treat others, they hear you.

I believe in middle schoolers. I believe that they think they are good people. I believe that they want to do their best, most of the time.

And, it's not always that easy. They also want to push boundaries.

And think adults don't "get it."

And they don't really want to be told how to feel.

Empathy and perspective-taking are part of the still-developing prefrontal cortex.

So any conversation you have with your kid about kindness/unkindness has to be about a baseline of everyone deserving dignity no matter what. Everyone.

Rosalind Wiseman, as we discussed in the last chapter, talks about, as opposed to respect, which must be earned and is conflated in kids' minds with the concept of compliance, dignity is the idea that everyone has the same inherent value. It is much more constructive to say: you must treat that person with dignity – and discuss what dignity looks like with your middle grader.

And, we can do better, too. As adults, we are privy to the many unkindnesses that our children share with us. And we don't say anything. We ourselves can be more direct, modeling and encouraging our kids to be as well. Not out of a place of anger, but out of a place of care and correction – out of a place of support of community. We worry we will break community and our children worry they will break community by "getting someone in trouble."

But when an unkindness has occurred, the community has already been broken. It can't be repaired unless next steps are taken. Talk to your kid and make sure they know that they deserve to be treated with dignity. The hope is that they have a strong enough sense of themselves to be able to say to someone, "You crossed a line." That they can speak up for themselves or someone else. And if they can't, they can go to an adult. Hard stuff.

Talking to your kid about: Is this a thing? Middle graders are often not sure whether they are upscaling or downscaling their problems, and they aren't sure if an adult needs to be brought into the conversation. Make sure you have this conversation with your kid: if they aren't sure if what is happening is a thing, have them check! If it is a thing, good thing they checked. If it's not, then no harm no foul. But better safe than sorry. Win-win. Wait. What is a thing?

Always make sure your kid knows what constitutes a thing. Middle graders struggle with right-sizing the scope of a problem. They need to know that if someone is being hurt, has been hurt, is going to be hurt, or is in danger – to themselves or someone else, then they must tell an adult. This is about safety. And safety is always the most important thing. Always. And they need to know you are always there. No matter what.

Topic: About Overwhelming Emotions

For all that is happening visibly and invisibly during puberty, so much is happening in the brain.

Middle graders need to know about the brain so that they can contextualize the feelings that become overwhelming during middle school.

Because feeling flooded and overwhelmed is worse when you don't understand why and you don't know when the feeling is going to end.

While we delved into the brain and how it works in Chapter 2, the following is worded to share directly with your middle grader.

You have two main parts of the brain that control how you feel and what you do:

- ◆ **The Prefrontal Cortex:** One of those parts doesn't fully develop until you are 25! It's just starting to grow. It makes up just 17% of your brain. It is called the prefrontal cortex. It's in charge of the stuff involved in self-control. It's also in charge of organization and executive functioning. That's why things like that can be challenging (Wolpert-Gawron).
- ◆ **Reactive Brain/Automatic Brain:** The reactive brain/ automatic brain, also called the limbic system, makes up the rest of the 83%. It's in charge of immediate responses. Fight or flight – that kind of thing – so you don't have to think if you're being chased by a bear. And now, meet our special guest!

The Amygdala

The amygdala is like a really good friend who sticks up for you all the time but thinks everyone is out to get you so gets upset at the smallest thing.

In middle schoolers, the amygdala is easily triggered because of the hormones activated during puberty Because the amygdala is part of the limbic system, it isn't weighing the pros and cons of reacting, so sometimes it reacts to stuff it doesn't need to react to. Even if you don't want to get upset, or don't think you should get upset, logically don't think something is a big deal, you can still experience an amygdala hijack. This raises levels of cortisol and adrenaline in your brain.

Which makes your body feel like it is under attack. That's when you might start breathing fast, your heart starts pounding, and your hands feel clammy. You feel awful. And, the amygdala's next-door neighbor is the hippocampus (it looks like a little seahorse, aww), which is in charge of learning. And that part doesn't work well while the amygdala is super upset. So it's important to calm the amygdala down before trying to get anything done. The good news is that the amygdala *can* be calmed down.

Calming the amygdala down can look like breathing deeply, walking, and crying can help too – actually – is a release. Journaling can help, or talking to someone who can calm you. But it is important to know that the feeling is yes, overwhelming, but manageable. It's because of that amygdala thing in your brain that would save you from a bear – it is looking out for you – you just got to chill it out again (Holland).

Knowledge and tools go a long way to help a middle grader take control of a process that so often feels out of their control. Each kid is unique and their coping strategies for a hijacked amygdala will be different. You will sometimes still need to point out to your kid that it is happening, "Seems like your amygdala is on fire right now. It's making it hard to do algebra right now," but it's another tool in their toolbelt and provides context for their reactions.

Topic: About Grief

Middle graders have trouble matching their response levels to the challenges that they experience. They can overreact or underreact.

So when something really difficult does happen, it's important to show them that their intense feelings may be very valid in this situation.

Often, they are used to people telling them that they are overreacting.

If they've experienced a loss, or a trauma, or an intense event, let them sit with their feelings.

And you can sit with your middle grader.

Help them to name and describe how they feel.

Normalize all the different ways they might be feeling.

And make sure they know that you take their pain and grief seriously.

And that you are there for them.

Seek support for yourself if you are grieving so you can be in a position of support.

Situation: When They're Shut Down

Likely, your kid used to go to you when they were upset. They'd tell you without you even asking – even the smallest things. But middle graders have become self-conscious.

At the same time, they are both extra reactive to things and also in the process of individuation. This is why now when they get upset, many middle graders may act like a cat would: retreat, close off, hide, and go inside – both literally and figuratively. They are learning new coping skills and trying to figure out how to handle themselves and all their new feelings.

Sometimes being inside themselves seems safest. So with a shutdown kid, as much as you want to, you won't be able to get them to open up until they've had some time to melt a little bit. They aren't trying to shut you out – they don't know how to respond. They might not be able to respond. The key is waiting. This can be hard. Our impulse is to want to talk to them. So we talk.

But instead, they need a short list of things:

◆ Time
◆ Physical comfort
◆ The knowledge you are there – so tell them: "I can see you aren't ready to talk right now, but I'm here when you are ready"

And really, actually wait.

You might need to wait a while. In the meantime, you can do things that will show you are there and that you see them: you can bring them something to eat, a favorite blanket, or a pet, or turn on a show they like in another room.

Sometimes they are shut down because they've made a mistake. So you might think: I don't want to reward them for this. But it's not about reward, it's about regulation and trust. They might be nervous to tell you. You can tell them you will help them through it no matter what.

Then, when they seem calm, you can say: "Tell me what's going on. Would you like me to just listen or help you problem-solve?"

And they may not want to share. If you are sure they aren't in a bad place, then that might be OK.

They need to know that they are allowed to have their own things. And you don't want them to hide their emotions because they are afraid of you "making" them share what's happening. Because there will *always* be something.

And they won't tell you everything. Nor should they. But you want them to tell you the important stuff.

They will know you're always there – that you can hold any feeling they have – and that is everything.

Situation: When They Messed Up: The Time Machine Conversation

Everyone feels intense shame and regret at points in their lives. These feelings can be so overwhelming that often a bad situation can be made worse while trying to avoid them. If your middle grader is experiencing these feelings, it can be helpful to have a time machine conversation.

Validating the feelings: "Sometimes when I do something I regret I feel awful and wish I had a time machine and could go back and change it." They will often feel very "seen" by this. It's a thought they may have had themselves but hadn't necessarily articulated.

So now you have an opening: "We don't have a time machine, unfortunately, so I am wondering what the next best thing is... what could help this situation?" Often the first answer will be "nothing," but with time and space, they can begin the process of fixing (the best they can) what has been broken.

Situation: When They Cross a Line

When upset, your middle grader may say things to you that aren't particularly kind.

They might even cross a line.

Don't take it personally, but don't just take it either.

In the moment: be calm, but firm. "I can tell you're upset, but you may not speak to me in that way."

They are trying things out, and you are safe.

Wait until they are calmer (this is *imperative*. This is the difference between a full-blown escalation and whatever the opposite of that is) and *then* discuss.

You can tell them how it felt when they said that. Remind them that you expect them to treat you with dignity AND respect. And if they aren't feeling the respect part at the moment, at least dignity.

When they are calmer, they will hear you and will understand there are lines they cannot cross – even when they are angry.

Situation: Dealing with Disappointment

When your middle-grade kid is disappointed: perhaps they didn't make the team they wanted, maybe they didn't get the part in the play they thought should be theirs. They didn't get invited to something. They didn't win the award they were hoping for. They didn't place in the race/match. The list of things that can be disappointing is endless.

It can be as hard on the parent/grown-up as it is on your kid. Make sure that the disappointment is coming from your kid and not how you think your kid feels/should feel. Sometimes they are more resilient than we expect.

And sometimes they are less resilient than we expect. It's our job to help them build that feeling of resiliency. And they won't build it without some uncomfortable experiences of not getting something that they were hoping for.

First off: validate their feelings. It does suck (or another word, but in cases like this, middle schoolers can feel seen when you use unexpected language – even a minor curse word...then they know you know it's important to them – dependent on your family norms) and that you wish it was different too. Ask them how they feel in their body. What they are afraid of. What they think will happen now.

Sometimes the disappointment is twinged with embarrassment or a feeling of being less than. You are there to remind them that they are much more than making a team, getting a part, etc.

If they are worried about what others will say or think: practice with your kid something to say that feels genuine but sets a boundary: "Yeah, I wish I'd made it, maybe next time." Share with them that the way they handle disappointment can impress other people – as much as getting the thing they wanted.

And all of this to say: being there and listening doesn't necessarily make the situation feel better. Time will do that. Being there doesn't hurt though. And they know you're there no matter what. However, reflecting on how they feel and how to manage the next steps will allow them to do the same the next time they are disappointed. Because it is a part of this life. And as much as we hate watching our kids experience it – it is making them stronger.

Situation: When You Need to Correct/Re-Direct Your Kid in Public

It will not come as a shock that middle graders are very self-conscious. Especially when they are with their grown-ups.

There are ways you can help them monitor behavior goals, or give them corrections in front of others, without infringing on their dignity.

This is important to keep your relationship with your middle grader strong through the challenges of this age. They are self-conscious and they think everyone is looking at them – judging them.

So if there is a need to give correction or help them meet expectations in front of others, it can be very useful to have a pre-agreed-upon signal. A signal allows them to feel in control of the situation, and they will more likely be able to take and hear the correction.

If they are embarrassed or upset, they aren't going to respond to any corrections or redirection anyway. Their amygdala will be highly activated. So to respect their dignity AND be able to guide your middle grader, signals can be a great tool.

Any signal or signals need to be pre-agreed upon with your middle grader. It is best if THEY come up with it.

You can have a conversation beforehand:

"I know that it upsets you when I tell you not to do something/do something when we are in public."

"Let's come up with a signal or sign so that you understand what I mean, but no one else has to know."

It can be a small touch on the shoulder, a hand signal, a word, or anything. Bonus points if it has some humor in it to lighten the mood.

It's not foolproof. Middle graders will be middle graders. But it is a tool in the tool belt. And they will see that you respect their dignity.

Situation: After You've Argued/When There's Tension/They Are in a Bad Mood

It can be a challenge to break the tension with a middle grader if they aren't in a good mood, or, even worse, if you've argued.

If you expressed your frustration, once you've had a chance to breathe, model how to make amends. That goes a long way in reminding them that you aren't perfect either, and that they deserve dignity, as do you – and the hope is that your apology will be reciprocated from a place of sincerity.

Here are several tried and true strategies to connect to your middle grader when you might need a reboot:

- ◆ Connect them with a younger child: kids this age are still kids. They are often their best selves when they are around younger kids (probably not siblings).
- ◆ Approach with humor. Easier said than done, but a well-timed quip, inside joke, or quote from a favorite show can often break the tension.
- ◆ (A more subtle approach.) Turn on a show you like watching together in the background and hope that they will come out, like a cat.
- ◆ Take them out to eat: Often, the way to a middle grader's heart is through their stomach. They *may* open up and share a bit more about what's going on with them once they've eaten something. Having one-on-one time doesn't hurt either. This helps them to regulate and to feel seen and can go a long way in filling up their emotional tank, too.
- ◆ Notice them doing something good. But be genuine and specific with your feedback. don't overpraise: they can sniff out insincerity real quick!

Logical Consequences and Getting Back on Track, Together

There will be times, perhaps around technology limits, or something that happened at school, when your middle grader will have made mistakes. Often these mistakes come with logical consequences of their own:

If they get angry at their friend and say something mean, their friend is angry at them. They will need to apologize and repair that relationship.

If they didn't do their homework and now need to stay home from the mall to finish, that is a logical consequence, and with a small amount of reflection, they'll learn from it.

Making mistakes is part of growing up. And, not just growing up. It's part of being a person.

Dr. Ginsberg in his American Academy of Pediatrics 2023 book, *Congrats – You're Having a Teen!: Strengthen Your Family and Raise a Good Person*, suggests creating a contract with your teen to discuss the cause and effect relationship of pre-determined freedoms and privileges with similarly pre-determined logical consequences. This way they are expected, agreed upon by both parties, and gives the agency to the teen – reminding them that their actions do matter and if they want a certain outcome, they can affect that possibility (230).

Consequences should not be doled out because there is "supposed to be a consequence." They are helpful only in so far as they affect change in the behavior or thought process of your middle grader. Change that means something and is lasting. Almost all of the consequences I could remember my parents giving were disconnected from the original infraction – the same goes for school. The times our class had to stay after during recess, had to run laps, or I had to put my name on the board. Of course, there are exceptions. The times that are burned into my brain – when cause and effect were too connected to separate. But it made me think about this need that we have for a consequence for every infraction that happens. I've seen children ask about what is going to happen to the child who has wronged them with a gleam in their eye, asking what the other student's punishment will be. What is their consequence? As if the consequence is the end. We've emphasized the wrong piece. Of course, there *are* consequences. Real ones: like people knowing you messed up or that that friend is upset with you. You need to make it up to them and then you have to do better next time. People might not trust you in the same way. And there are times when a consequence is logical: "You break it you fix it." But to create a consequence out of thin air to fulfill a magical need for a consequence doesn't help anyone learn anything.

For some grown-ups of middle graders, there is the worry that if they don't make an impression when their kid makes a mistake and don't make it clear that they're upset, their child won't get the message. Trying to make kids feel something, shaming them into feeling something or a similar strategy, or using guilt to elicit action, may perhaps result in a change in that moment, but will have no lasting effect on character development, and may encourage your middle grader to hide their infractions from you in the future.

Kids tune out adults when the adults are upset at them. It hurts them, so they just don't take anything in. And they learn to deflect. To hide their errors. To minimize responsibility. They also don't want to feel like their parents have that much control over their feelings and their lives. It feels too big and out of control.

We have the most impact when we help them realize that taking responsibility is hard but expected.

And that only happens if they are open and not already shut down to our words.

If we can reframe for our kids: yes, there are absolutely logical consequences for their actions. That's how life works. But the best people, the bravest people, those are people who take a deep breath and say yes. I did this. I accept responsibility. That is the mark of a good person. The kind of person who learns from their mistakes.

Because we judge people more on how they respond to things, and less on whether it happened in the first place.

In this relationship, we are the grown-ups. Being the grown-up actually can take some of the onus and the responsibility off being the perfect parent. Because if we think about what is going on, that's part of our worry. If we don't make that impression this one time, if we don't get the message across, we worry so many possible outcomes might happen. What will our child turn into? What if they don't ever understand?

We need to beware of the siren song of future parenting and remember that we have a wonderful middle grader in front of us right now. A middle grader with all their potential, who is learning to individuate, and take responsibility, and the least we can do is to pull back a bit and give them some.

(This chapter skips "Talk Middle Grader to Me" since the bulk of the chapter is that very topic, and probably for the best since we'd run out of space for how many times "do you want me to help you problem solve or to listen?" would be mentioned.)

6

Academics and Middle School: A New Frontier

Personal Inventory

Do you remember the content you learned in middle school?
What model of school did you attend for your middle grades
   (approx grades 5–8)?

6–8?
K–6?
6–8?
7–8?
Pre-K/K–8?
Pre-K/K–12?
Other?

How was your experience?
How was the transition, if you had one, between your last
   year of elementary school to your first year of middle school
   (either fourth to fifth, fifth to sixth, or sixth to seventh – the
   fifth to sixth transition being the most common)?

What subjects did you enjoy?

DOI: 10.4324/9781003527831-7

Was it easy?

Did you struggle?

If you struggled, what parts were challenging, the content itself or the general concept of school/homework?

If you struggled did you get help?

Did work ever feel too easy, boring, or uncompelling?

On a scale of 1–10, how motivated were you by academics?

1   2   3   4   5   6   7   8   9   10

What would happen if there were behavior issues at school? How was discipline handled?

Did you often "get in trouble"?

Did you have relationships with teachers that helped you to feel connected?

What did learning look like and feel like?

How involved were your grown-ups?

Do you remember what you thought the *point* was?

Increased Academic Expectations

As you'll remember from Chapter 2, the brain is doing a LOT of work at this time, and it's only natural that the work ramps up for middle graders as well. But if you'll also recall, not everyone is at the same stage at the same time – PLUS all those amygdalas, all those feelings, and all that puberty all in one place can make for a tumultuous few years. What academics end up looking like is different for each person, different at each grade level, and different at each period of growth, which either does or does not happen to correspond to the grade level the student is in. According to the *Scholastic* article "Academic Learning Among 11–13 Year Olds," "For some children, the transition from elementary school to middle school is bumpy, for it involves expanding their world, increasing their independence and upping their responsibility" (2019).

Both the skill level of middle school academics increases as does the depth and breadth of the content. Students are responsible for more: not just in terms of holding onto what they learn and demonstrating in varied ways across disciplines that they know it, but also in terms of being responsible for getting themselves to a place where they can budget their time in order to *learn* the information, create the project, write the lab report, compute the math problems, think through and answer the questions, discuss the permutations, write the essay about that complex idea, and organize their thoughts, BUT also need to do it over chunks of time about approximately a week, or a week and a half, or two week periods in which they ALSO must figure out how to balance all of their extracurricular commitments and responsibilities at home.

If this seems like a lot, it's because it IS a lot. And while middle schools, whether they begin in sixth, or have a different start year, all work to scaffold (helping students by unpacking what's needed for success in a particular skill area and working on the components step by step to develop mastery) students (Wills et al.) in their ability to organize their materials digitally, physically, and psychologically, the truth is that the transition to the at least partial autonomy of middle-grade academics can present a challenge to many students.

If it were just the academic and skill piece it would be easier to parse, but there are other factors to consider. For the academics and skills: students this age, as they are now reaching their formal operations stage, can make inferences from primary source documents in history and discern bias of historians in their social studies, humanities, and history courses. This, as you can imagine, can really deepen the level and complexity of discourse, should students be intellectually engaged. Students this age can infer the properties of a substance in chemistry based on its behavior in an experiment and then write up all of this in a lab report using scientific writing that is similar to, but not the same as, the writing that they use in their language arts classes. In language arts, they can look at literature symbolically, inferring meaning from the word choices authors used to discern what connotations may be there, hidden under the surface. They can make a claim and then back this claim up with evidence, reasoning, and analysis. They can do complex mathematics, symbolic math, and solve problems with abstractions. Of course, they can't do all this in their first year, but at some point, it all comes together.

But the fact that they DO this is pretty impressive!

Motivation Makes a Difference

I've tipped my hand twice now, maybe you've noticed. In the previous section, I said "This, as you can imagine, can really deepen the level and complexity of discourse, should students be intellectually engaged." *Should* students be intellectually engaged – and then, in the Personal Inventory, I asked: "How motivated were you by academics?"

These questions are paramount at this age.

Take all the puberty, the brain stuff – the expanding gray matter and with it the increased risk-taking, plus increased skills, and even with the most interesting content and skill building in the classroom, the course content isn't always what is primary for middle graders. They are often focused on the other, albeit important and interesting, things happening in their lives that are decidedly *not* academic.

Some students are very motivated by academics. They don't require much more than just being in the environment. They may love learning, they may love the simplicity of knowing that if they complete a task to a particular level of competency they can achieve x result, or they may be motivated by external factors. There are some students who have low levels of motivation and require a great deal of push to get to the motivation level that some students start with innately.

There are intrinsic and extrinsic motivations: intrinsic motivation comes from inside and is when a student wants to engage and do the work for reasons within them. Extrinsic motivation means they are focused on an external reward of some kind, be it a grade, a prize, praise, or meeting other particular expectations. Educators tend to support intrinsic motivators as being more desirable, but researchers have also indicated that extrinsic motivation can be useful in moving students to motivate when used mindfully. But the long and short of it is that increasing middle graders' motivation in academics is paramount in order for them to be able to remain on the high school graduation path.

Some ways to help increase student motivation that classroom teachers can use at this age are to have positive learning environments, to make the subject matter relevant to their students, and to create projects that have impact in real life (Ruiz).

All of that to say, if your student is not motivated, it doesn't mean that all of this isn't happening in the classroom, it may just mean that your middle grader is, at this moment, not in a place where they can take all of it in. If we go back to that idea of the amygdala and hippocampus: the hippocampus is not going to be able to work on all the learning stuff if the amygdala is triggered all the time. Or perhaps that class isn't on their motivation list.

Grown-ups of middle graders get reaaaaaaaallllly frustrated here. Because it is very challenging to motivate the unmotivated. Educators are pretty good at it, but there gets a point where, and if you have a kid that has been at THAT level of unmotivated, you're doing more than they are, or you're lifting more than they are, and the teacher is doing more and lifting more – well, it's time to pass at least some of that lift back for them to share.

You might think. Give up! How can I? You can't. You're right. But, you also cannot do middle school *for* them. So, what you *can* do is set the expectation and share in the support, but as a coach. You say: the expectation is that you go to school, that you pass your classes, that you continue your education (or your expectations as you see them). I expect you to ask for help, and to accept the help you are given. You can listen, ask questions, and problem-solve, but the expectation stays.

And with all that, your middle grader's motivation might still be a challenge. A drop off in motivation at this age is, in part, expected (Pickhardt).

Sometimes part of the challenge *is* the very transition to middle school – or the challenge of the executive functioning that comes with the transition. There are a lot of things that they are dealing with that are competing with the academics. All of those things are like arrows coming at them – they are fighting them off at all turns.

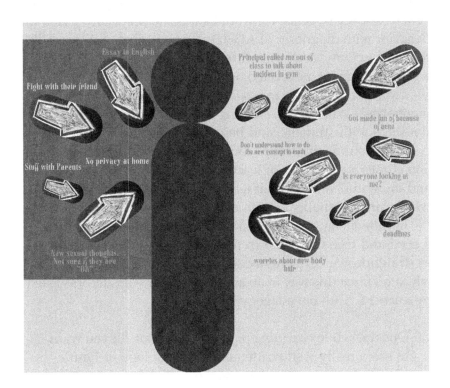

It's good that the challenge and interest ramp up in middle school: because if it didn't, it would be even harder to get middle graders motivated!

Classroom Expectations and Unexpected Behaviors

Another challenge students often find when they transition to middle school is a mismatch between their behavior and the expected behavior of the classroom. Indeed, their behaviors can be "unexpected" and not particularly, as an educator might say when trying to be diplomatic, "conducive to the learning environment."

In addition, the format of middle school specifically can lend itself to increased issues in behavior challenges as students move from class to class, discipline area to discipline area, teacher to teacher, needing to create a different schema and adaptation plan for six or seven teachers instead of one – which makes students prone to unexpected behavior *particularly* challenging (Caldarella et al.) – especially since we would expect to see a correlation in behavior with diagnoses of ADHD and behaviors of distractibility, hyperactivity, and immature behaviors, which are the gateway behaviors to unexpected behaviors.

Proactive classroom management (Caldarella et al.), behavior monitoring (Wills et al.), creating expectations and strong relationships with students, and being consistent go a long way in creating a strong classroom community and better focus for all. Sometimes it's a matter of teachers figuring out how to connect and show students that their teacher is invested in their progress, which can be a challenge at this age.

In elementary grades, positive reinforcement for behaviors is a tried and true tactic, but in middle school, praise isn't always as straightforwardly accepted. Jennifer Gonzalez, the educators' educator, put it this way in an anecdote on her website, oft-visited by teachers, "Cult of Pedagogy":

> One day while returning papers I called out, "If you want to see a really well written essay, take a look at Emir's." My thinking was that they would be all, *Wow, if a cool guy like Emir writes well, then I want to do that, too.* Nope! Emir looked at me like I just took his wallet. And for the rest of the year, he turned in crappy writing. It's not that the praise was unwelcome, it was the public part he didn't like. If I wanted him to keep writing well, I should have kept quiet about it.
>
> (Gonzalez)

It's not that students don't *want* praise, but they are picky about how they want it. Remember, they think everyone is looking at them already and you don't know about the narrative they've created in their head and what it says. Praise delivered across the room isn't a good idea at this age, non-specific praise will not be taken at all, or worse, will be perceived as insincere. Praise that is specific, brief, individualized, focused on effort, and not gushy, will be best taken by middle graders (Schneider et al.).

Additionally, the relationships that students build with their teachers at this age can do a lot to make a difference in student motivation and improved behavior. Advisory programs can help students to be accountable for their success and each aspect of their development – and can help make sure they feel that there is a grown-up at school on their team ("12 Recommendations for Middle-Grade Success").

1. But what can you do as the grown-up who is NOT in the classroom? You have a lot of partnership opportunities to support the teacher, your middle grader, and the whole class-room community.
   ♦ Your middle grader is prone to hyperbole – just remember that at all times.
   ♦ Being a middle-grade teacher is challenging because of, well, all of the above.
   ♦ Your kid's teacher is an expert and most likely very much wants the best for your middle grader – AND has a class of other middle graders.
2. Your kid can learn how to be a better person from being in a classroom with other kids who are also learning how to be better people.
   ♦ Whether your kid is the unexpected behavior kid or the kid who is coping with an unexpected behavior kid, these interactions will make them a better human person. Don't seek to eliminate the interactions. Seek to improve the *quality* of the interactions.
   ♦ If they are the unexpected behavior kid, listen to the teacher and ask their expert opinion. Ask other experts. *You* are an expert on your kid. *They* are an expert on kids in this particular context.
   ♦ If your kid is the coping kid, reflect, reflect, reflect. What could they do differently next time so that other people's actions don't affect them as much? Do *their* actions play a role in the dynamic (they almost always do, at least a little)? This is a good time to practice flexing that empathy/perspective part of their brain.

3. Approach with curiosity – always.
   - ◆ Ask, listen, problem-solve: WITH your middle grader AND teachers

It might feel like most of your conversations with your kid's teachers are about their social, emotional, and behavioral development – depending on what your middle grader is working on – and that's OK. Sometimes that is the most important work a kid is doing in the middle grades, and the academic work isn't going to get done if that base, foundational, and most vital work is neglected.

Executive Function: An Achilles' Heel of Many a Middle Grader

The term Executive Functioning is a catch-all for all of the skills and behaviors that people use to make plans, execute their goals, and organize their lives, spaces, time, work, activities, and even maintain their friendships. Some of these skills are self-control, problem-solving, working memory, and inhibition ("Executive Function"). If you are looking at this list and thinking to yourself, that sounds like 17% brain stuff from back in Chapter 2, you are NOT wrong! Those are skills solidly within the prefrontal cortex's purview and therefore middle graders are not going to necessarily just waltz into middle school and have them at their fingertips ready to go.

Instead, these skills develop concurrently as their brains develop, as their bodies develop, and as they grow in their abilities to think and reason (Jacobson et al.).

So you can imagine, then, that of the most challenging pieces of the move from an elementary setting to the complexity of the middle-grade situation is the management of everything: the time, the stuff, the projects, the homework, the friends, the extra-curriculars – all of it.

They want increased autonomy and some of it they are ready for, but the organization of their life needs to be scaffolded – think of it as preparing your middle grader to ride a bicycle.

You don't start with a dirt bike on trails. Whether you want to start with one of those balance bikes or old-school training wheels, that's your choice, but middle-grade students need support with learning how to look at a week and piece out their assignments into chunks based on their availability depending on their family and extracurricular and other school commitments (just writing it sounds complicated).

Middle school teachers and advisors will help with this, but middle-grade students need a grown-up to help with this a bit – depending on the level of organization that they start with. Some kids have more ability in this area than others and some need more support.

A word about the chart below. Each middle-grade student will develop on their timeline, see Chapters 1–2! So these are approximations and depend on your child as well as the expectations of the school and the norms of your community.

The next few mini-sections will go through these in more depth.

One of the most important things to remember, as you go through these sections, is that Executive Functioning Skills are *skills*, and therefore can be learned, worked on, practiced, and taught. A person will have a basic starting point that may or may not put them at an advantage or disadvantage, but as discussed in Chapter 2, with Growth Mindset, these skills are not fixed and students and students grown-ups can work toward success in these areas.

Schools also play a role in creating plans that address scaffolding and learning executive functioning skills for middle graders, as EF skills are trainable and moldable (Cumming et al.).

Additionally, and perhaps unsurprisingly, connections with teachers and close monitoring of social-emotional connectedness, according to a research study conducted with a community of low-income students of color in the Southwestern US, has a positive effect on executive functioning, as well as math and reading achievement (Lemberger et al.).

All of this to say, middle graders are going to need some help learning to ride the bike.

AUTONOMY SCAFFOLDING FOR MIDDLE GRADES

	FIFTH GRADE	SIXTH GRADE	SEVENTH GRADE	EIGHTH GRADE	GROWN-UPS
NIGHTLY ASSIGNMENTS	Needs grown-up help nightly to check on assignments due the next day- or check that they were completed. Weekly check necessary.	May need grown-up help nightly to check on assignments due the next day- or check that they were completed. Weekly check necessary.	May still need a grown-up to check to see if work is completed. Weekly LMS check-ins help to make sure that homework is up to date.	Weekly check-ins can be sufficient as long as work is getting done. If there is a lapse or assignments not turned in, then nightly checking may be necessary.	Imagine they're riding a two-wheeler. They're going to fall off, but you'd prefer they not break all their bones. So keep your hands in that awkward kind of holding position over the bike.
LONG TERM PROJECTS- STUDYING	Many long-term assignments in 5th are done in class. 5th graders need help parsing out studying. Take the test date and walk it back a week or so and carve out time with them.	More long term projects in 6th. They need support piecing out projects into parts before the due date/not leaving to the last minute. Same with studying.	Should have a better idea how to do this in 7th, but still need reminders. It's a good idea to talk through it with them. Don't do it FOR them, though.	They will be more adept at independently organizing their time long-term, but may still procrastinate. Be their study-buddy and support.	Help by communicating clearly what appointments they might have that interfere with school. Talk through how YOU chunk out larger projects.
COMMUNICATION	Need a grown-up to model and write email to teacher with them when they will be absent or missing school, or need to complete make-up work.	Need a grown-up to write the email with them still if they will be absent or missing school, or need to complete make-up work.	In 7th grade, they can write the email and grown-ups can check it to make sure email etiquette has been followed.	In 8th grade, they should be able to write the email themselves and their grown-ups can confirm with them that they've sent it.	This is a life skill, being able to communicate clearly. Making sure that they do so and following through on it shows them that you value this skill as well.
ORGANIZATION	With help, they should be able to keep up with the organization system (physical) and LMS that the school requires.	They may still need help with organization, both digital and physical in 6th grade. This is an area of challenge for some students. If this is an area of challenge for yours, they may need additional supports.	They may still need help with organization, both digital and physical in 7th grade. This is an area of challenge for some students. If this is an area of challenge for yours, they may need additional supports.	In 8th grade, even students who struggle with organization have often found something that works for them. Keep looking, use all tools that seem helpful.	Not all tools work for all people. Don't force the tools that work for you onto your middle-grader. Let them try out things that work for them. They will find something that works. Even if it's not pretty, if it works, it works.
EXTRACURRICULARS/ APPOINTMENTS	Many 5th graders have extracurriculars, but usually they don't interfere with homework, yet.	6th grade is when things start getting dicey with extracurriculars and homework. Students who are very scheduled need to know what their weekly commitments are in order to parse out their week. They need their grown-ups help for that.	7th graders who have practice in balancing a lot of afterschool stuff and curricular work are getting better at it, but they still need help piecing it out. Make sure they know in advance what is coming up and sit each week and plan.	8th graders will have made some decisions about where they want to speed their time. They may have cut things down, or added things. They will still need to make sure that they have enough time for all of their activities each week.	This is one of the hardest parts of organizing a middle-grade life and it's a whole family affair. Plan it together and discuss it together so that everyone supports each other.

Time Management

Many students need support with time management. They may have a bit of time blindness – they may not know how long five minutes actually is. In order to help them with this, make sure, when you give them time limits, or how much time it is until something, to give them that exact amount of time. This will help them calibrate their internal understanding of the amount of time it takes to do something with how much time – actual time IS.

TIme management in middle school has a few parts. Students need to learn how to answer the following questions:

1. How much time is time? (See above. How long five minutes *actually* is.)
2. How long a task will take vs. how much time you *personally* will need to complete the task (which requires a prior understanding of your pace of work)?
3. How much time do you have to do a task each day and what time chunks can you do it in? For example, a free homework period. Or will you use your free periods to chat with your friends? (Priorities.)

All these working together are quite complex for students, and, remember, in most middle schools they need to do this for multiple classes.

1. Talk to your middle grader about time management and its challenges. See how close both of you are to calibrating your concept of one minute or five minutes.
2. Then, have them choose one of their homework assignments and try the middle time-management question: have them gauge how long they think it will take, and then see how long it actually takes. See what the difference is.
3. Finally, and this will also be part of organization, with the info they have from 2., figure out how long they need to do everything they need to do that week. It's a mental math problem for homework that they didn't know they had!

Calibration and Reflection

Reflection is one of the ways that students can make these very important connections between their own actions and the results of their actions.

Fifth and sixth graders are just making the connection between the time and effort they put into their work and the grade/result they earn. As they become more aware, help them reflect: How long did it take you to do that? How did you feel about the grade you earned? Is there something you would have done differently? This helps them to calibrate their efforts to the result. Not everyone can do this naturally.

Seventh and eighth graders are more aware of their responsibilities but still may require reminders. They are in the process of developing their ability to stay organized, but their proficiency is not yet foolproof. Academically, by seventh and eighth grade, most students will have gained a better understanding of themselves as students. They likely have a system in place to organize their work, though it's likely not perfected yet. They may require less parental support or check-ins, depending on how well their system is working and their current level of follow-through. Occasionally, disagreements with parents may arise as seventh and eighth graders seek increased autonomy in their education – sometimes without realizing their continued need for support. Providing places in their lives where they can exercise independence outside of school is important, particularly as academic challenges intensify.

Organization

There are quite literally, I bet, a billion kinds of organization systems, but they really only need to do one thing. Well, two things, because there are two main kinds of organizational systems that your middle grader will need and both depend on what their brain needs and what their school requires.

1. Organization of physical stuff and physical space – we'll call this one "**Stuff Organization**."
2. Organization of Things to Do, Places to Go, and Time – we'll call this one "**Life Organization**."

Stuff Organization

Experts suggest having a workspace particularly JUST for doing homework, if possible, so that your middle grader associates doing work with that space. The space should be somewhere they can focus. They may need noise-canceling headphones to be able to focus if they need to share a space where other things are happening. Supplies are important:

Some things your middle grader may need:

- Flashcards
- Pencils
- Highlighters
- Colored Pencils
- Erasers
- Pens
- Folders

This is where it will be important to note what the school requires your middle grader to have.

In Laurie Chaikind McNulty's book, *Focus and Thrive: Executive Functioning Strategies for Teens* suggests:

> Start with designating a place for each of your items. Label folders, alphabetize your file cabinet, tidy your bookshelf, and assign boxes for your school supplies. (Hint: taking things out of the packaging and putting them into bins makes the space a lot more manageable.)
>
> (McNulty, 40)

Chaikind also suggests scheduling some time to organize your space into your calendar each week.

Which brings us to the next category.

Life Organization

Here's where your middle grader will need a planner, or an online calendar program should that suit them – but something that your middle grader can piece out their time in chunks and write down/type what they need to do each day, plus any appointments, chores, other commitments, family stuff, friend hangouts, time to organize their space, clean their room, and do all their school work.

They may also need a checklist so that they can get that amazing feeling of crossing things out and marking things off once they finish.

You, as an adult, might have a system that works for you. You might have an app or a physical planner or calendar you've been using for donkey's years that you love. You can suggest yours, but cautiously. Even if it does work for them, they might reject it outright just because it's yours – that's a middle grader for you.

Look through a bunch of options. There are always lists compiled of best planners, and schedulers, online or analog. The best system is the one that they WILL USE.

Communication and Self-Advocacy

One of the ways that students can learn how to advocate for themselves is by practicing it. And most self-advocacy is done using communication.

Some students have specific academic needs they need to advocate for: they have particular accommodations, an IEP, a 504, or a particular medical need and they need to be able to communicate clearly about what they need and when they need it.

But communication in terms of self-advocacy in the middle grades – and beyond – is more than that. It is making connections with teachers, communicating about absences, asking for clarification, asking questions about homework or classwork, or wondering about the timing of a make-up test.

Now, of course, there is a limit to this. A student needs to be measured with these things, and that is also why the middle grades are such a great time for learning how to communicate through email and the timing of how to approach a teacher.

When do you approach a teacher? Well, the real answer is – it depends on the teacher, but in general:

1. Not right before class.
2. Not in the hallway.
3. Not before they are going to go to the bathroom.

4. **After class your middle grader can approach and ask: When would be a good time to chat? I have a question about** _____
   .

Or, make an appointment through email:

Dear _____

I hope your week is going well so far. I know I missed Monday's class and I need to make up that quiz on polynomials. Can you let me know a good time I can come by to go over it?

Thanks,

_____

Because they'd already let their teacher know in advance:

Dear _____,

I hope you are having a great Wednesday. I am planning to be absent next Monday for a trip to my cousin's wedding, so I will be missing your class. Besides checking (Insert whatever Learning Management System/Online Classroom Program used), please let me know if there is additional work I should complete.

Thank you so much,

_____

In terms of these types of emails, in fifth grade, they are going to need help with every step of it. They won't even realize they need to write one – same with sixth grade. Write the email with them in the fifth and sixth grades. In seventh grade, they can write the email and you can check it before they send it. Eighth, you can check in and just make sure that they did it.

Good habits.

Habits that will serve them well as they go on to bigger places, even bigger schools with more kids to contend with. They will need to be able to talk to adults, to be able to get clarification, ask for what they need, and to approach teachers when necessary.

Self-advocacy in the middle grades can also be standing up for what they believe in, which is so very important, and, in this age of people saying things on the Internet that they'd never say to someone's face (more on that in Chapter 7), so very important to add to the discourse. But so is the tone and package in which they add it. One of the adages I share with my middle graders is that their ideas deserve to be heard, and one of the ways that they can more easily get their ideas heard is if they package them in a way that will make people want to listen and not immediately discard them because they seem like they are an old moldy sock or something.

Communication comes in many forms and it's a practiced skill.

Strategies for Learning: Metacognition

Metacognition is the process of thinking about your thinking. There are different strategies, but each involves a reflective process of students using their newfound skills of abstract reasoning to think about their brain processes. Students with strong skills in metacognition can learn more and perform better than peers developing in this area. Julie Dangremond Stanton et al. in a CBE Life Sciences article compiling research on metacognition found that:

> Students with well-developed metacognition can identify concepts they do not understand and select appropriate strategies for learning those concepts. They know how to implement strategies they have selected and carry out their overall study plans. They can evaluate their strategies and adjust their plans based on outcomes.
>
> (Stanton et al.)

The 2021 article discusses the key factor of collaboration in metacognition – that discussion is an important component of this work. For middle graders, this can especially be the case as they are already primed to be social.

Mindmaps are another way of thinking about thinking. A mind map is creating a map of the way a person is seeing and creating connections. A learning technique that is being used in schools, once students master it, it can show all of the ways the brain processes information, including words, colors, and numbers, see the relationship between ideas and what might look like unrelated concepts, and interdisciplinary ideas – connecting disparate parts of the brain visually. It is also a way to get students to think about the way they are thinking and the way their brain works (Arulselvi).

Teachers have used this in the classroom as a way to support student understanding of complex mathematical procedures. One teacher noted in the study that especially for students who were having trouble with concepts, she was seeing success with the process of them writing out their thinking processes instead of just answers (Lemley et al.). In math, this might look like answering a question: What strategies did you need to use to solve that problem? How did you start? If you made an error, how did you fix it? All of these questions make more visible to the students the way that their brain is working to do all this work that it's doing.

Even in terms of organizing life, or maybe especially organizing life, thinking about how things are going, and reflecting on processes, can be especially helpful to mark progress. Assessing how "things are going and making adjustments as necessary" (Chaikind, 83) is part of the process of growing into the self. Nothing happens overnight in middle school.

Differentiation and Acceleration

While the academic challenge of transitioning to middle school can be a challenge, as I mentioned earlier, if both the content and skill level didn't ramp up the way it does, middle graders would likely disengage even more. There is a complexity required once students begin to reach formal operations – engaging them with engaging material.

And some students are ready for this, and more. Perhaps they've been identified as gifted and are ready for content and skills above their grade-level peers. One important thing always to keep in mind: there are few cases, gifted or not, in which every aspect of development is in lock-step together and this is especially the case with students whose academic potential and abilities are beyond what is expected for their grade level. This means that there could, though not necessarily, be deficits in other areas. A student who is gifted, or advanced in academics, could struggle in their social interactions. It is important, whenever looking at a particular child's needs – that the whole child be addressed – not just their academic potentiality.

Differentiation – an education term described by Stanford's Center for Teaching and Learning as, "Teaching in a way that meets the different needs and interests of students using varied course content, activities, and assessments" ("Differentiated Instruction"). Differentiation, done well, attempts to reach each student where they are and help them to achieve curricular goals despite those varied skill and ability levels. It does require teachers to be trained and practiced in its implementation (Stanford, CTL).

But, done well, differentiation can go a long way in meeting the needs of a gifted learner in a mainstream classroom as teachers can hone in on both depth and breadth in content and skills and find topics of interest for them to pursue. It is also a tool for teachers to support students who are struggling or who have specific learning differences, which we will discuss in the next mini-section.

By its nature, differentiation isn't streamlined by school district or state – and neither is the pace or way in which to advance gifted or accelerated students. Math tends to be a place of easiest acceleration as the concepts don't become dicey or developmentally inappropriate in the way literature can be. The skill of reading isn't going to prepare an elementary-age student to be able to read a text that is about adult themes that go beyond the schemas they currently have developed (Sparks).

All of that to say, these are school-based interventions. The question for a grown-up of a student who is gifted or accelerated academically is: Are they thriving at school? (Or as much as a human being thrives during the process of transforming and changing from a child into a more adult human.) Are they enjoying the process of learning? Do they have social bonds? If the answer to these things is yes, then things are good. Students who are gifted often seek out stimuli and enrichment – and as a gifted student's grown-up, you can support these endeavors and interests as interest – not just skill – is a strong predictor of their continued success and continued learning (Sparks).

Learning Differences: A Reframe and Opportunity for Perspective-Taking

It can be hard enough to be a middle grader, much less have an additional challenge. There are a couple of different ways to look at that – and by the end of this, hopefully, we can do a full reframe. Already, students think everyone is looking at them because they are just developing a little bit of gray matter in that prefrontal cortex that is helping them see that others have different perspectives, but unfortunately, what they've gleaned from that is a concern about what others' perspectives are of THEM (Anthony, "Cognitive Development").

So if they have an additional challenge (and you, by extension, as the grown-up supporting the middle grader most definitely have an additional challenge to manage as well), they are likely going to be concerned that this will make them "different" in some way or make them stick out.

But remember this: they also think they are unique, which, yes they are – but they have that personal fable thing going – where they think their experiences are unique and their feelings are unique. It's not a bad thing to capitalize on here.

And, with a reframe – stick with me here – you've got a kid with a challenge, reframing their challenge into a narrative of courage and superpower, AND you've got a bunch of other kids' learning perspectives and empathy by learning about other ways of looking and being in the world.

That's the goal. So let's talk about how to get there:

You might have a kid who has autism, who is 2E (twice exceptional), who has a serious medical condition, who is deaf, who has a learning difference, who has social challenges, who has

ADHD, who has mental health challenges, who struggles processing information, and the list goes on. Some people have to work harder at the world than others. Often, the world isn't made for differences. In my experience as an educator, I've found that the more empowered with knowledge, tools, and skills a student with any kind of difference is, the better they fare. Self-knowledge is a big deal. And owning who you are is even better.

This transparency also helps other students to be more empathetic and understanding and gives all students the tools to collaborate with all types of people. Each one of us has our strengths and challenges; just some kids' challenges are a little more obvious than others.

Getting to the above requires your child's educators to help facilitate these conversations, for your student to be equipped with information, and for people to be, well...understanding. And it can be challenging for parents to be OK with sharing diagnoses, etc. Indeed, there can be stigma and implications there. And let's face it, people aren't always understanding.

But it's been my experience, with almost every kid, that the students who own, know, and work with their differences do better. They do better at the things they struggle with and they do better emotionally and socially. And people are usually willing to be more understanding when they have a fuller picture.

In the last mini-section, we talked about gifted kids. There is a group of gifted kids who are 2E, or Twice Exceptional, meaning that they are both gifted and have a learning difference. That learning difference could be neurodivergence (someone whose brain processes differently), on the autism spectrum, ADHD (attention deficit hyperactivity disorder), dyslexia (a neurological condition making reading challenging), or dyscalculia (a learning difference in mathematics which can affect understanding numbers or problem-solving). Sometimes it can be a challenge to recognize 2E kids because of what could be thought of as contradictory diagnoses (Tahmaseb).

With a student who has been diagnosed with learning differences, there will be student study team meetings through school to set goals and make sure that everyone is on the same page and path to success. As I mentioned in the last section, differentiation is an important way that academic expectations and standards can be met or exceeded while still making sure that a student with learning differences is within their Zone of Proximal Development and not stretched too far or not far enough.

Talk with your middle grader's teacher – not just about their IEP (Individual Education Plan), 504, or accommodations. Talk about to what extent your student is comfortable sharing about their challenges and what skills they've acquired as a result of those challenges – whether they can talk about how their world is a little bit different – and in what ways that is unique to them and the things they've learned as a result.

This is the reframe. They are already primed to hear their own stories as narratives. Allow them to reframe their challenges into stories of overcoming something. The word overcoming is ongoing – it doesn't imply their struggle is over or everything is wrapped up in a bow. What it does imply is they have skills other people don't, and that they are, indeed, unique in that.

Philosophers and Children

I don't think that anyone can put it in starker terms than Jennifer Gonzalez of the Cult of Pedagogy in her article "8 Things I Know for Sure about (Most) Middle School Kids."

One minute you're having a deep philosophical discussion with them about the symbolism in a Robert Frost poem, they're *really getting it,* and you can almost see them maturing right before your eyes. Ten minutes later they're making armpit farts and asking if it's OK to drink the water from the fish tank (2014).

I have definitely had a kid who would have asked if it's OK to drink the water from the fish tank – they are just delightful, ridiculous, goofy, and deep as heck.

Every kid is a philosopher. At my school we've been working with a program called Philosophy for Children – and it's amazing to see the way in which students, given the space and time to think and ponder the world's questions, can ask themselves what the meaning of existence is – whether there was time before time began, or what existed in our consciousness before we existed.

We can have an amazing philosophy discussion, and then it's time for lunch and the kids go out and run to the lunch line – even though we've asked them literally a billion times to walk – and then later go out to play. And when I say go out to play, they *really* go out to play. Less the eighth graders and seventh graders, but the fifth and sixth graders still play tag or elaborate games of hide and seek with stakes that I don't understand. They are children. They are philosophers. They are academic and developmental contradictions all at once.

They are middle graders.

Talk Middle Grader to Me: Chapter 6

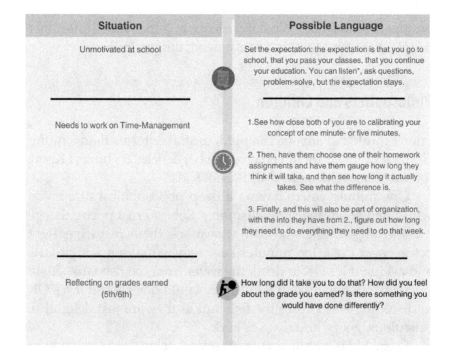

Situation	Possible Language
Unmotivated at school	Set the expectation: the expectation is that you go to school, that you pass your classes, that you continue your education. You can listen*, ask questions, problem-solve, but the expectation stays.
Needs to work on Time-Management	1.See how close both of you are to calibrating your concept of one minute- or five minutes. 2. Then, have them choose one of their homework assignments and have them gauge how long they think it will take, and then see how long it actually takes. See what the difference is. 3. Finally, and this will also be part of organization, with the info they have from 2., figure out how long they need to do everything they need to do that week.
Reflecting on grades earned (5th/6th)	How long did it take you to do that? How did you feel about the grade you earned? Is there something you would have done differently?

Situation	Possible Language
Student needs to send emails to teachers with grown-ups help	Dear _____ I hope your week is going well so far. I know I missed Monday's class and I need to make up that quiz on polynomials. Can you let me know a good time I can come by to go over it? Thanks, _____ Dear _____, I hope you are having a great Wednesday. I am planning to be absent next Monday for a trip to my cousin's wedding, so I will be missing your class. Besides checking (Insert whatever Learning Management System/Online Classroom Program used), please let me know if there is additional work I should complete. Thank you so much, _____
Helping them think about their thinking	What strategies did you need to use to solve that problem? How did you start? If you made an error, how did you fix it?
Your middle grader has a challenge: learning difference/medical issue/other	You have challenges other people don't and so you have skills other people don't, and you are, indeed, unique. Your challenges do give you particular super powers

7

Our Collective Challenge: Technology, Social Media, and the Middle Grades

Personal Inventory

It's harder to do a Personal Inventory about this chapter, at least for me. When I was in middle school, it might as well have been a different world:

> If we needed to write a paper we wrote it by hand. There were stages: a rough draft stage, an editing stage, and then a final draft stage where we copied it over with edits – this time with a pen.
>
> All information that our grown-ups needed to know about us was sent home in weekly printed newsletters, through the mail, happened at parent-teacher conferences, or was communicated in phone conversations with teachers or administration.
>
> If you wanted to know what grade you were earning, you were in the dark unless you were keeping track meticulously of the points possible vs. the points you earned, or you asked the teacher.

DOI: 10.4324/9781003527831-8

If our parents needed to get in touch with us during the day, they left us a message in the school office.

If we needed to know what the homework was and we didn't write it down, we needed to call people in our class until we got to someone who was (1) home and (2) knew what it was.

If we wanted to talk to a friend on the phone we needed to call them and usually talk to an adult gatekeeper first, asking if that friend was available to speak.

If we wanted to watch a television show, we either needed to watch it then, or record it to a VHS tape to watch it later. DVRs and TiVos replaced this technology later.

If we wanted to take a picture and have it come out immediately we would need to have a Polaroid camera, and film for those was expensive. Otherwise, you would need to take your film canisters to a developer and get the prints back in a week or so, depending on how much you paid for the turnaround.

If you wanted to watch a particular movie, you rented it from the video store. You had to physically go there and acquire it and then return it. Be Kind, Rewind.

Video games were collaborative, but you had to be there in the room with people – you could go against your friends in various fighting games, take turns on levels in Super Mario, or play Mario Kart, but until a bit later, you couldn't play remotely.

If you *did* type your work, you had to keep saving it or you'd lose it!

We passed notes in class.

If you liked one particular song off an album, too bad, you had to buy the whole thing.

I list these things not to be nostalgic for those days, to bemoan them, or to grouse about the way things are now. I have always been a technology adopter with an interest in what it can do to improve things, and make things more interesting or creative – and when I was growing up I thought the technology we had was pretty sweet because it was what was available. And it was the 1980s and so everything had a kind of tech-cool sheen like that.

All of this to say, I don't know HOW to feel about our kids growing up in this technological world. It's overwhelming, it's scary, it's powerful. They have so much POWER with these technologies, and they are so young. Especially in the middle grades. They don't know how to use that power and they need our help to be able to learn and practice how to be responsible humans with it. They need to learn how to make healthy boundaries for themselves in order to have a balance between technology and reality. In order to appreciate the world as it is vs. the world as it could be.

Technology isn't good or bad. It's neutral. But what we do with it and how we use it certainly can be. And the way our kids use it can be as well. But because we are the grown-ups, and the adults in the room, the onus to be better, to do better, is on us. Because it's on us to model for THEM, and to teach them to do better.

Perhaps this Personal Inventory should be a bit more about NOW.

Let's restart.

Personal Inventory Take 2

If you have one, how often do you use your phone per day?
1–2 hours
2–4 hours
4–6 hours
6–8 hours
8+ hours

Do you follow recommended procedures that we all know about and put it away about 30 minutes before bedtime?
Y/N

Do you sleep with it outside the room you sleep in?
Y/N

Do you have dinner every night with your phone in another place?
Y/N

On a scale of 1–10, 1 being unconcerned, 10 being super concerned, how concerned are you about your own technology/phone use?

1   2   3   4   5   6   7   8   9   10

Social Media and the Middle Schooler

The middle grader and social media is a tricky combo. It's not an inevitability that a middle grader has access to *social* media, per se, though, in this day and age, it's impossible to avoid all media in general.

Social media offers a curated world of bubble gum, glossy, shiny, new, idealized living – and unattainable existence that even those purporting to live it don't have.

It is hard for adults, who logically understand that it's unattainable and unreal and that what they are seeing is ultimately curated for public consumption, to not feel a tug of envy in their hearts when they see that perfectly clean house, or new device or gadget, filtered face, curated moment, beautiful vacation, amazing relationship, or exciting adventure. It may seem like we are not living our lives in the best way we can, and we want to strive to have more, do better, get more, and *be* more. It's the siren's song of endless advertising and capitalism. The pull of this kind of media is so strong, even with a lifetime of experience, that humanness and vulnerability around our perceived flaws and our hopes and dreams for our lives, we can still fall prey to a filter selling a product promising to change everything. Imagine, then, how impressionable middle graders, middle graders who think that everyone is looking at them, middle graders whose bodies are changing and are surging with hormones in differing quantities, middle graders who are not necessarily comfortable in their own new skin yet – imagine how vulnerable they are to this type of thinking.

This is not the only thing that social media, technology, and the internet have to offer, but it's often the first foray many middle graders make into it. It is communication, but it's also peacocking. It's connection but it's also isolation. It's community but it's also exclusion.

Mental Health and Technology

The stats aren't looking good, folks.

Adolescence is already a period with an increased risk of mental health challenges (McLaughlin and King) as the changing brain and hormones in puberty, along with increased pressures, can create situations of stress. Technology and social media use add to this stress in a myriad of ways and these work together to add to that stress, which leads to an increased likelihood of mental health issues, namely depression.

The UK Millennium Cohort Study on 10,904 14-year-olds published its results in 2019. It studied the interplay of sleep, self-esteem, and online harassment on depression scales in young people.

Many young people sleep with their phones near them. Sleep issues are linked with mental health – it is certainly a possibility that notifications and the pull of FOMO (Fear of Missing Out) of whatever conversation might have happened or might be happening affects sleep in students.

There is also the relationship between the curated images and filters and students' self-image and self-esteem and how they feel about their own bodies. Comparing one's real body to a filter is an impossible comparison to win.

Then there are instances of online harassment, when there is targeted harassing communication that is derogatory and damaging to relationships and students' psyches (Kelly et al.).

The data from the study indicates that the interplay of these things, greater social media use corresponded with a greater likelihood of depression, poor sleep, and lower self-esteem, with girls experiencing more depressive symptoms than boys (Kelly et al.). So there are three issues to manage here correlated with the use of technology and social media, besides the umbrella issue of depression: sleep, negative relationships, and self-image.

To drive this point home, a study conducted in 2023 found statistically significant improvements in perceptions of appearance esteem and weight esteem in students who reduced their smartphone use by 50% (Thai et al.).

These results are compelling for any grown-up who works with middle graders, heck, for any person who has a phone and a body and brain who compares themselves to other bodies. Social media, for all of the sometimes positive things it can do, has brought with it unintended consequences with it. And these consquences can create problems, especially with middle graders, as Jonathan Haidt says in his book, *The Anxious Generation*, "The costs of using social media, in particular, are high for adolescents, compared with adults, while the benefits are minimal. Let children grow up on Earth first, before sending them to Mars" (Haidt).

Haidt has become a voice for limiting social media use for teens, delaying when students get a smartphone, and encouraging parents to have a greater involvement in their children's online lives. These arguments have resonated with parents, though there are certainly critics of Haidt's claims citing that his data doesn't go far enough. There are two particular counters to Haidt that are relevant to middle graders. 1. addresses the argument the Internet and social media are overall detrimental to teens. There are many teens, middle graders included, who have found online communities that offer support and social interactions that they may not be able to access at home, at school, or socially. And 2. addresses the argument that waiting to introduce social media and other technology until high school could deprive students important opportunities to learn how to interact with the Internet and social media in a responsible way, teens need to be taught and have chances to practice – when they are more open to parental involvement – such as when they are in the middle grades, rather than when they are in high school (Schiffer). Haidt's suggestions assume a child's home life is enough of a haven and that a teen won't need to look outside it to get support. Certainly, to smartphone or not to smartphone, and to what extent, is going to be top of mind for many middle grade parents, and middle graders themselves. It can be a challenge to parse what to do, and middle graders do not make it easier as they often want more responsibility in this area than they may be ready for.

A question to always ask yourself is: what is a balanced approach? None of us want our own kids to become the case studies, yet we need long-term data to help us make thoughtful decisions about how much, when, and in what ways our middle graders should engage with or step back from what technology offers. Our guiding principle should be to focus on the children and the situations right in front of us, rather than reacting out of fear because we read a study or book and started worrying that we were "doing it wrong" (again), like the debates around tummy time or cry-it-out –wondering if we're making lasting mistakes. Read the reports, the books, and listen to the experts and then do the best thing for your middle grader and your family. Like teeth brushing, the best answer is the one that makes it happen. The one that works. There is a paralysis that can occur with technology sometimes where it feels easier to do nothing or to keep looking for an easier way. The way is *always* going to include conversations with your kid and a realistic expectation that these conversations will need to keep happening. There is no magic recipe that will solve the tech problems. But let's put a pin in that.

But Everyone's Doing It!

This is a refrain that every grown-up of every kid has heard since the beginning of time, probably. It's always whatever the new thing is.

But now it's about tech: When is it time to let them, get a phone, a watch, or get a social media account?

Well, this is a complicated question with a complicated answer.

A phone: it depends. It depends on why you want your middle grader to have a phone. Is it because you live far from school and you want them to be able to contact you in an emergency? Is it because they have begged for years and you're tired of hearing it?

Is it because they are responsible and you've drawn up a contract? Is it because you'd discussed them getting one at 13 and that birthday is approaching? Again, Haidt weighs in in *The Anxious Generation*: not until age 14 (Haidt).

A watch: many watches can do what the phones do. So see above. Depends on what they are using it for and why they need it.

Social media: I'll tip my cards on this one. I don't think most middle graders (ages 10–14, grades 5–8) need social media – at least the common social media apps. Some kids have channels where they build Lego and show it off, or group chats with their friends which can be in a different category. But if they are posting a picture of what they do on the weekend and then tagging friends and waiting for likes, that is likely not good for them. It's going to hurt those excluded, and it's not good for their own development or mental health either. Haidt's stance is clear about social media as well, not till 16 (at least) (Haidt).

One argument that students often use when trying to convince parents to agree to get them a phone is that EVERYONE in their class has one. This is a blatant attempt to make you feel like they are left out because they know that that is a button for you and you will feel bad and be more likely to acquiesce. But, unless they are in eighth grade or ninth grade, this is *highly* unlikely. They'll *say* it, but it doesn't make it true. There are always families and grown-ups of middle graders who, for whatever reason, do not choose to give their children a phone. This group is, as expected, of a higher concentration in fifth grade and gets smaller as the students get older, but there are almost always still students in eighth grade who don't have phones. Also, there are flip phones available.

A legitimate question: When their whole social world, nay THE whole social world is online, are you doing a disservice keeping them off?

Sure. A little. But it can be mitigated with real-life interactions and as long as you're willing to make that happen it's fine. There are also ways around letting your middle grader talk to their peers without giving them their own phone. For example, they can chat through email, or on another device. Or, if you are a lucky grown-up, you too can be part of the "Elf the Musical Group Chat" on YOUR phone like I was for a whole winter once, since my son didn't, and still doesn't, have his own phone.

And, perhaps the most important for any grown-up who has heard the incessant whine of "But everyone's doing it!"

The answer can be simple:

"Every family has different rules. In our family, we do things this way."

Filters and the Curated Lifestyle

Cosmetic work, including plastic surgery, or less invasive procedures such as botox, used to come with a stigma. Whether this is fair or unfair is not for this book to discuss. However, what is true is that this stigma is dissipating due to social media. Young people are more likely now to view cosmetic procedures such as lip fillers as more commonplace.

A survey conducted by Anne Mette-Hermans in 2022 found that while not all young people are planning on getting cosmetic surgery, there is a correlation between those who would be more likely to consider it with those who follow influencers who have more procedures. Additionally, the study also found a correlation between young people who used filters to edit their pictures and embellish their faces digitally to their willingness to undergo cosmetic work.

Dr. Emanuele from the Child Mind Institute points out that for middle graders who have spent a lot of time curating their own image online, it's not just who they see and want to emulate – they may also look at their own life – the one they've curated online and feel frustrated because who they are on social media isn't the person they are in reality (Jacobson et al.).

As we discussed above, depression is a vulnerability at this age, and the perfect social media profile and life can be a facade for a problem internally. And Dr. Emanuele points out as well that while social media may contribute to these issues, they are doubtfully the root cause, but they most certainly don't help (Jacobson et al.).

Anonymity and the Dangers of Not Looking Someone in the Face

It will not come as a surprise to you, grown-ups of middle graders, that there is a significant correlation between anonymity and uncivil behavior on the Internet. In one study, 53% of comments posted anonymously were negative, compared with 23% of non-anonymous neutral or non-negative comments. Perceptions of anonymity are also linked to cyberbullying behavior, in other words, if people think that they have anonymity, they are more likely to engage in cyberbullying. There is even research that shows that anonymity at one point in time can predict cyberbullying behavior later (Dawson).

Middle graders sometimes struggle with saying nice things to people's FACES. They struggle with saying nice things in group chats when the person in question is there.

Make sure your middle grader knows these two things about anonymity on the Internet:

1. **For safety:** never give your name, address, or location to anyone on the Internet.

   So how to square with your kid the challenges of being anonymous and not sharing their name? Talk to them about Digital Etiquette, Digital Ethics.

2. **You can't remind your kid too many times at this age that what they say on the Internet needs to be at the standard of how they would speak to someone face-to-face (or better).**

3. Richard Culatta, author of Digital For Good – Raising Kids to Thrive in an Online World uses the educational concept of place-based education – the idea that learning is tied to the place in which it is taught – when he explains that kids need to be explicitly taught the strategies and tools for being kind in the real world because those things don't always translate to being kind online. In other words, in order for our children to be able to be proper humans online, our children need to be taught to be proper humans online: "If you teach a kid to be, you know, a good, healthy, respectful, engaged human in the physical world, those strategies for how to do that look different in a virtual world. And so we have to teach them overtly…even when we have people who are being very healthy, engaged humans in the physical world" (Culatta).

What Goes There, Stays There

Most middle graders know that what goes on the Internet will, indeed, stay on the Internet. In fact, if you went up to a middle grader right now and asked them to finish this sentence, "What goes on the Internet _____ _____ _____ _____" (stays on the Internet). They KNOW it, but because they are middle graders they forget and don't really have a concept about long-term consequences and are more concerned about what they are doing in the short term. This, as we remember from Chapter 2, is a result of the not yet fully developed prefrontal cortex, so, while developmentally appropriate, it still needs to be addressed because, as we've established, what goes on the Internet, stays on the Internet.

Hopefully, whatever stays on the Internet for our middle graders isn't something as monumental as those stories of universities or employers digging on the Internet and finding something untoward, and then rescinding admission or employment.

How do we prevent this?

There is a lot of digital education that happens in school in the middle grades. They will learn about the digital footprint, copyright, what websites to trust, etc., but this one is a good one for grown-ups to take a larger role in since the purview is outside of school, too.

Make sure that you have this conversation occasionally. They mean to remember, but they forget. Monitor their socials once they are allowed to have them. Have a deal worked out that you won't comment or post if they are worried you'll embarrass them (sorry to break it to you, but they'll find another platform anyway that you won't know about – they get away from us so quickly.)

The best way, because of this slippery bit, is to just keep discussing with them how important it is. Talk about the digital footprint. Talk about what you yourself post and what you *don't* choose to post and why. Ask permission before you post their pictures to model consent.

Remind your student that their future self doesn't want to deal with the negative online choices of their middle-grade self. And that they need to do that self a favor and keep things copacetic.

Screens and the Home

Up until 2010, when parents said "screen time," they meant television. But since the advent of the smartphone and tablet, the ubiquity of these things, and the way they've made their way into the hands of children, screen time means a whole different thing.

Since parents were concerned about the first kind of screen time, it's not a reach to think that they would be immediately concerned about the second kind of screen time. And the way that the applications for these screens have been created, they work to make the user keep coming back. At this point, screen addiction is a real issue.

As this is a new phenomenon, experts haven't reached unanimity on symptoms and diagnosis of screen addiction, which makes it complicated to diagnose. But, in terms of what experts are seeing, younger adolescents with poor self-concepts are more likely to suffer from Internet addiction. Gaming is one of the most usual activities seen in adolescents with this addiction, though not the only one (Lozano-Blasco).

Parents struggle to create boundaries with their children on how much screen time they will have, when, and how often. It feels often, like the children are insatiable, if they get some time, they crave more. Some parents have reacted by getting off screens entirely. The next few mini-sections will look at aspects of tech in the home.

Trade-Offs: Connect, But Make It on a Screen

danah boyd, author of *It's Complicated: The Social Lives of Networked Teens*, discusses the movement of teenage hangouts from physical spaces, in malls, on corners, at parks, in front of stores, in alleyways even, or in the woods to often almost exclusively online spaces that are meant to, if not mimic those spaces in their physical resemblance, mimic them in their utilitarianism (boyd, 202–203). Researcher Jean Twenge has found that young people's interactions are increasingly digital (Twenge and Spitzberg, 2020).

Not only are their screens a space to interact – to see and be seen, meet new people, or people they know only online, get new outfits ("they're called skins, MOM"), and change their look or avatar, but often these games are played while being on a headset talking to friends they know from "real life." Often, many kids are playing these games at once. So many, that this can create an issue if your kid isn't allowed to play a particular type of game, or if they aren't allowed to have screentime during a school week, or at a specific time, or after a specific time, etc.

This original retreat from physical spaces was quite likely due to the increased concern of stranger abductions of the 1980s (Williams), which relates to reason number two: **ALL Prevention, ALL the Time** – that parenting is such a challenge. There is this concern that if something *could* happen, then we are bound to make sure it *doesn't* and the best way to make sure it *doesn't* is to ban whatever it is outright. And now, we have online spaces for adolescents to retreat *to*.

Now, is that also the case for screens? boyd would say that it doesn't leave our kids with much of an option, since the public and private spaces are mostly online. Indeed, part of being their age, though an older middle grader, is to see and be seen – like at the mall – what is now social media.

They are connecting, and making connections, but they are doing it through the medium of the screen (boyd, 203).

There was some helicoptering, one could say, now they are safe, they are in their rooms. We've provided them with tools to stay safe there. Indeed, there was a global pandemic and they took their lessons from there as well. But now, we are surprised and concerned that they don't want to leave.

Perhaps this is hyperbole. But our middle graders use their screens as an extension of themselves. They are a communication device, and different from the way that we mean it. They use their devices almost as a language. They communicate with them, interact with them, and then they look up and communicate in reality. They are multilingual and they can move back and forth effortlessly.

This by no means is meant to say that our middle graders should always be on their screens, but, it is some larger societal and historical context for how we got here and how *they* got here.

And where we might go from here.

I Don't Want to Fight Anymore: Creating Boundaries around Tech with Your Middle Grader

So what is a grown-up to do?

How can a person create boundaries when for your middle grader their social life is connected to the screen (not to mention everything for school is on those dang things – but that's for another section)?

Every family is going to have a different style or different goal. As I mentioned, some families are done with the whole business, going screen-free.

Others have worked out boundaries.

Pediatric and adolescent medicine suggests the following steps:

1. Distinguish between school and recreational screen time (both should count toward the total of [whatever you decide]).
2. Conduct a family meeting where everyone suggests their ideas: no phones during dinner or before bed.
3. Create a balance of on/off-screen activities.
4. Use apps and tools to both monitor, block, and create focus time (specific apps are always changing, what is most important when choosing an app is the features you want it to have and what you are looking for it to do, not *which* specific app it is).
5. Discuss *why* you have these boundaries and rules. Middle graders are more likely to comply if they understand why. For more on why, see the sections above (sleep, mental health/depression/negative self-image).
6. If changes need to be made, specifically reducing screen time, make them gradually as this could be met with resistance.
7. Be a model. Lead by example. Go back to the Personal Inventory. If you are anything like me, you likely didn't score the way you would have asked your middle grader to behave. We need to do better and model the online and digital behavior we want to see in our middle graders (Mastruserio, 2023).

If you are met with resistance about screentime in the moment, you can reiterate the plans you have come up with:

1. "We created a plan together and we aren't going to change it on the spot. If we want to change it, we need to discuss it as a family and that isn't going to happen now."

2. "I can tell that you're upset with this boundary, but right now it's my job to enforce it. We made these rules together and agreed as a family."
3. "This is a complicated thing you are asking for and I cannot discuss it with you on the fly. If you'd like to discuss it together, let's make a time when we can give it the time and space it deserves" (paraphrased from Dr. BeckyGoodinside).

There are apps that will monitor your kids' online behavior – but proceed with caution, Devorah Heitner, Ph.D., author of *Growing Up in Public: Coming of Age in a Digital World*, says, "If your child cannot express how they really feel to you, but reaches out to friends about mental health issues, monitoring them too closely might be cutting them off from their support system" (33). While some experts aver that monitoring is an absolute necessity in this day and age, monitoring of kids' texts, like the reading of an old-school diary, or asking their friends who they have a crush on, while they've happened to have gone outside to take out the trash, can certainly also be seen by a middle grader as a breach of privacy and boundaries.

For some parents, this is a non-negotiable condition for allowing their child access to the Internet. If this is non-negotiable for you, be sure your middle grader clearly understands the exact boundaries of the monitoring. This reflects a long-standing tension between teen autonomy and privacy versus parental oversight, now playing out in the digital world. The goal is for your teen to develop discernment, common sense, and ethical behavior online –earning greater autonomy and trust as they demonstrate growth in these areas.

If you allow your student to have a chat going, or a phone, or social media, it's a learning experience for you both. Not just a learning experience about the tool, but a learning experience about boundaries, about how to have challenging conversations, about how to be an upstander in a chat group, to advocate for what they need, to connect, to get politically involved – and all of the important conversations that need. And depending middle grader – again, these are still young kids – it is important for them to know that even though you think they will do a great job with these things I've mentioned above, it's not quite their time yet. "BUT WHEN *IS* IT MY TIME?!" I can just hear it. I'm sorry. If all else fails, you can always pull out the tried and true, "When I say so." Don't actually do that. That will not help.

Going Screen-Free

Far be it for me to tell you what to do, but I don't suggest going *completely* screen-free. Why? Well, because your kid needs to have some modicum of ability to monitor themselves on a screen. If they have NONE, they're going to be like me when I went to my friend's house and went crazy on the Pop-Tarts because my mother didn't let me have processed sugar till I was eight. There is a skill in self-reflection, a skill in learning how to be uncomfortable stopping yourself even though you want to continue, a skill gained in learning how to balance screens with offline activities, real friendships in real life with real friendships online, and all of it. That balance and those skills are really important and will not be something your kid will be able to practice if they don't have any opportunities to do so.

Everything Lives There, Even Their Schoolwork

Schools overall embraced technology – after all, it did make writing essays so much easier. Truly.

But I get the feeling if you polled most middle grader's grownups, that they've about had it with tech in schools (Grose).

There is a model that thoughtful reflective school leaders and teachers employ when thinking about new technology to use in the classroom called the SAMR model. It is a hierarchy of neutrality to transformation – basically – did the technology DO anything different? Did it allow for a significant task upgrade or creative merits – all the way to transformative: Did the technology allow for a transformation of the task such that using it is worth it significantly?

Technology for technology's sake has always been a dirty phrase in educator circles – and the SAMR model is meant to guide the choices that educators make when emphasizing technology in the classroom. I say this not as a technology apologist, but to give a perspective – educators are either also (1) not as into the tech as you think, (2) being thoughtful, or (3) using it in thoughtful and purposeful ways.

But at the end of the day, this doesn't change the fact that even though schools, after a game-changing convincing *Atlantic* article in the summer of 2023 called for the removal of phones from campuses, most middle graders have a device, loaned by the school or at the school to use for school, or at home for use for schoolwork, or that is their own, that does everything a phone does and then some.

Now, are there some advantages to this? Absolutely!

◆ The essays, mentioned above. Always for greater collaboration on these papers and editing with the teacher and peers. Students can also remotely work on projects, slideshows, and other presentations. This can be very helpful, especially for students who live remotely or who lack transportation.

◆ Also, learning management systems, of which there are many, too many specific ones to count, but all have the same functionality: they can track assignments, grades, sports games, communication, and all that jazz. This is a double-edged sword, like many things. It can allow for greater parent involvement and oversight in the student's progress, AND it can also allow for great ownership and reflection on the part of the student. AND it can also lead to hyper-focus on grades. You can tell this has happened to a particular student when they come up to a teacher and say something like "I turned in this assignment and my grade only went up .24." So LMSs, some good things, some drawbacks.

◆ Organization: as discussed back in the last chapter, executive functioning is a challenge at this age. With a computer, it is hard to lose stuff. Though, my goodness, do they try. There are apps folders, email, and systems pre-built for them to take advantage of.

◆ Study skills too, there are systems that can help them already with retrieval strategies if they don't have a partner to work with. Computers can go a long way in helping them with this.

◆ They can create art, podcasts, and other media.

But if you're trying to set boundaries with screen time at home and your kid happens to use the same device for both, it can be quite a challenge.

A few suggestions:

1. Have a different place for recreational vs. work-time screentime.
2. Make sure they tell you when the transition happened so that you aren't counting "work-time."
3. Figure out whether work-time has to come first or not, otherwise, they'll equivocate about it forever.
4. Figure out a focus app that they want to use. Have it be their idea somehow.

Good luck.

"And You Say Multitasking's a Myth, Mom!"
– My Middle Child

Every time my son does two things at once, especially if one of those things is on his computer he will yell in my direction, "And you say multitasking's a myth, Mom!" Every. Single. Time. It's like he is personally offended on behalf of multitasking. He loves the concept of multitasking and has set out to prove that not only is it a thing, it's a thing *he* can do, and so, he says, can every kid in his generation.

Regardless of whether he can or not, middle graders DO multitask. You're liable, if you aren't sitting there monitoring your kid doing homework, to find them listening to music, talking to a friend, doing math, with a chat up, a YouTube window, and like maybe three other things going on as well. According to a 2018 study, 60% of students 10–15 reported multitasking. The study correlates multitasking with more negative academic performance and also takes more time to complete tasks if multitasking is a factor. Heavier multitasking, i.e., doing things with more complexity correlates with more negative results. The majority of similar studies bear this out as well (Soldatova et al.).

So, yeah. I win this round, kid. The data doesn't lie.*

*I really hope not. That would be really embarrassing for me.

AI, Trusting the Internet, and Thinking for Yourself

Some of the most important work that students can do on the Internet is to hone their critical thinking skills. In an online world that is increasingly full of deep fakes, fake news, artificial intelligence, and filtered images meant to look real, middle graders have a lot to sort out, and we can support them in that.

As part of digital etiquette and digital citizenship, schools will undoubtedly have lessons built into their advisory curriculum or their civics, social studies, language arts, science, or homeroom curricula about how to discern what makes a website trustworthy, what to look for, and how to check against a checklist and criteria.

Commonsense Media, a great resource for parents and educators in general, has a curriculum that includes, "Test Before You Trust" which walks students through things they should note about a website before they decide whether the information on it is valid.

- ◆ Are there a lot of pop-up ads?
- ◆ Are there a lot of misspellings?
- ◆ Does it look professional?
- ◆ Is it .edu, .org, or .gov? (CommonSense Education).

There are also lessons on how to check and verify information from more than one source.

AI

Artificial intelligence is everywhere and will continue to grow exponentially. We haven't even scratched the surface to see what the implications for education will be, but I can imagine that there will be some interesting adjustments made as a result.

For now, students need to be very careful with AI. They need to understand that anything that they get from ChatGPT or another AI source needs to be cited the way they would cite something they didn't write themselves.

Students this age also struggle with the idea of citing their sources – they understand they need to cite when they use a quote, but they have a harder time when they paraphrase. This is helpful information to know for the AI conversation.

The main tip for AI is to be aware of whatever the policy of their school is around using AI for their school work and follow it very carefully. They don't want to accidentally use it in a way that gets them into hot water if they didn't realize they weren't allowed to. **If they aren't sure, ask.** All of these conversations are to help them avoid plagiarism, copying another's ideas or words without permission. While it is, generally speaking, much better to make that mistake as a middle grader than it is a higher schooler or a college student, better to learn how to avoid it in the first place.

Some helpful ways TO use AI* can be:

♦ Proofreading and editing their work (if they are allowed to) the prompt has to be very specific. "Please proofread and edit ONLY."
♦ "I am brainstorming essay ideas for the book *To Kill a Mockingbird*, what would be some good themes to start with?"
♦ "Please remove all formatting from this document."
♦ "Please translate this into _____"
♦ "Please help me come up with a good apology for my friend. I _____"

*Carefully

AI is a powerful tool. Use it *with* them.

Balancing Act

All of this tech stuff is a balancing act. You will see that again and again in advice to parents and grown-ups of all ages managing this screen stuff. Balance.

It's easy to say and hard to do.

Before you completely despair because this is, indeed, a lot. And, indeed hard. Remember this: we are the first generation of parents raising children who have had this level of unfettered access to technology and the Internet and the tools to access it. We are the first generation to have to parent under these circumstances. We deserve credit for the work we are doing to put in place boundaries and guard rails to keep our kids safe considering all of the massive amount of information out there and the extent to which a whole bunch of it is not for children. We deserve credit for the work we've done to teach them moderation in their use and approach. We deserve credit for coming up with all those workarounds for all the workarounds that they came up with for our workarounds.

We deserve credit and we still need to keep working on it, of course.

But take that breath first. We are in this together. We will get through it together and this generation, the middle graders now and coming up will figure it out. They will have their own challenges with the next generation. But for now, this is ours.

When Your Kid Does Something Inappropriate on the Internet

◆ Keep calm.

◆ Ask what happened.

◆ Listen – because the situation may have been complicated and your kid may need to be heard for THEM to hear any messaging around this.

But regardless of complex circumstances, it doesn't change that they can't say mean/inappropriate things in chats/comments, threaten, impersonate, cyberbully, or any number of online infractions.

Once you have the context – at least as far as you can gather, then share that you expect your middle grader to speak to people online with respect – as you would expect in person – or whatever the unique circumstance is. The order of these things is dependent on your middle grader and the situation, of course, but some mixture of the following likely needs to happen.

And share with your middle grader. Since they are a middle grader, this is the time to make these mistakes. And they WILL make mistakes. The most important thing is to learn from them and you do expect this to be a learning experience. It is better, actually, that your middle grader makes a mistake of this kind and goes through a process of reflection and repair than doing something later when they are older – when the consequences are likely more dire and possibly irreversible.

HOWEVER, the mistakes they made shouldn't define them, especially if they go through the process of reflection and repair. But the way they handle it will show their mettle and will help them grow. A middle grader is still a CHILD. They are learning. They are capable of brilliance and immaturity at the same time. They have access to technological tools more powerful than they are likely ready for. It is our job to educate them, to reinforce what they should and should not do, to help them to take responsibility when they make mistakes, and to allow them to move on from their mistake if they make repairs and learning occurs.

And don't be afraid to ask for help and guidance from your community. Schools are very conscious of these issues and would likely proactively partner with you, or reactively work on repair with you and your student, and help to entrench the concepts of online etiquette and the importance of digital citizenship. CommonSense Media is also a good resource for information on children's safety and online behavior. It's a great big internet and we are all learning to navigate parenting with it and our kids using it – for the first time in history. Let's work together to help them.

Digital Etiquette

Agreement

If you are going to entrust your middle grader with a device, then I suggest having them sign a contract that enumerates the rules they will abide by and what the consequences will be of non-compliance. Whether they have a phone or not, they will likely be online regardless – almost all schools require students to be online!

See below for three different examples of contracts I created for my children. The first was before my oldest had a phone and was for him to have crystal clear boundaries for tech use. The second was for when we gave him a phone – note that his father and I also indicated what we would contract to as well. The third is a picture of three general principles I've printed (you'll note that we are *definitely* running out of ink) and, of course, discussed with the middle child since he now messages with friends. It's pinned by his bed and so far has been enough. For now.

Digital Footprint

Discuss the concept of a digital footprint and how even though they are kids, their online actions can have real-life consequences. Share with your middle grader the significance of being cautious about their online presence and its effects on their reputation and future opportunities (especially if they are an older middle grader and already thinking about their next steps). However, this is not going to be the most effective tack with middle graders as it is quite far in the future. It doesn't mean that you shouldn't mention it or discuss it, you should. Just know that your kid isn't going to say, "Shucks, Dad, you're right. I am going to be more careful about my digital footprint now since you and I had this discussion. I guess I don't need social media after all." The focus instead should be on conversations about ethical behavior and how to treat people in life and online. While they will still make mistakes – the expectation of a foundation of humaneness is there, along with the understanding that the online space is a different beast than face-to-face – more easily misinterpreted, more easily spread, and in many ways, much less forgiving.

Touching Grass
Help them find a balance between screen time and other activities. Work with them to come up with balanced habits, like taking breaks, managing time online, and fostering a positive relationship with their devices and all technology.

Privacy and Security
Make sure any device your kid uses has privacy and security features that you've vetted. Ensure they know that people can pretend to be who they are not and that they need to be careful and come to you if an interaction doesn't feel right.

Etiquette
Teach them how to write a proper email, attribute credit, and share that you expect them to be respectful and appropriate in all their online dealings. They should know that you expect them to act ethically.

Common Sense
Make sure you've discussed that not everything on the Internet is true! They need to think critically and carefully and not automatically trust everything they see and read. This is a time for them to apply those abstract thinking skills that they are beginning to flex in other arenas and apply them thoughtfully to the online world.

Example Contracts

Other Tech Type Contract

	Computer	iPad	Messaging with Friends
Time Limits	During free time OR after homework for a preset amount of time, not to exceed ___. On weekends for a set amount of time.	During free time	
Prerequisites	Homework & Chores	Homework & Chores	Homework & Chores
Limitations			No playing games you are not supposed to play. Messaging content needs to be appropriate and kind.
Permission Needed	Youtube, app store, any changes to settings/modificati onsAny live multiplayer games.	App store, YouTube, changes to settings. Any live multiplayer games.	
Consequence if rule broken	Sit at the table to do all school work. Nothing fun for x amount of time, commensurate to infraction.	No iPad except for piano-- time to be determined depending on infraction.	

Off-limits Regardless:

No night use of any devices. Obvs. No Fortnite or pugilistic games, no social media.

I, _____accept this contract on this day _____

Cell Phone Expectations

1	The phone sleeps outside your room at night and charges
2	No phones at the dinner table
3	Avoid bragging about the phone to friends (who may not have one) and brothers. Either don't use the phone in front of them or allow them to have a turn.
4	Take care of the phone- it is expensive. Don't leave it places and make sure that you keep it safe.
5	All school technology rules must be followed
6	You must communicate with mom and dad. Answer our texts and calls. Especially if you aren't at home. (not during the school day)
7	You need to keep on top of your homework in order to have this privilege
8	Keep positive relationships with the family and spend time in the living room with us
9	Your phone curfew is a half hour before bed - meeting and exceeding expectations regarding homework, behavior, and chores could give you more time, and not following expectations could result in having to put the phone to bed after dinner.
10	We will spot-check your phone. We expect you to text appropriately, not search for inappropriate content, stay focused while working on homework, and not develop online relationships with people you don't know. • Do not take pictures or video of others without their permission • Do not forward inappropriate content or content of others without permission • Remember that everything on the Internet is public and forever- do not post or write anything that you would be embarrassed your teachers and family would read (no social media) • Don't broadcast your location • Ask for permission to download apps • Don't respond to numbers you don't know or click on Spam texts, etc.

*These rules are subject to change

Mom and Dad rules:

Put phones to the side during family time (in the living room)

Ringers on if phones are to the side.

Only earphones while cooking/cleaning/working around the house

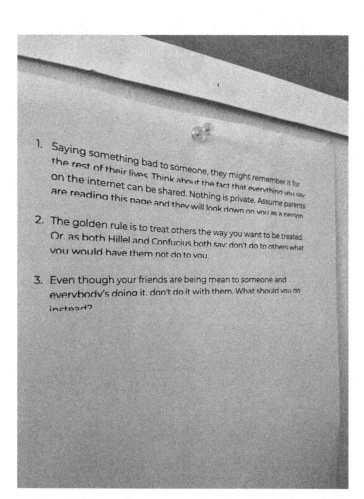

1. Saying something bad to someone, they might remember it for the rest of their lives. Think about the fact that everything you say on the internet can be shared. Nothing is private. Assume parents are reading this page and they will look down on you as a person.

2. The golden rule is to treat others the way you want to be treated. Or, as both Hillel and Confucius both say: don't do to others what you would have them not do to you.

3. Even though your friends are being mean to someone and everybody's doing it, don't do it with them. What should you do instead?

Talk Middle Grader to Me: Chapter 7

Situation	Possible Language/Plan
They want to know why they can't have ———— "But everyone's doing it!"	"Every family has different rules. In our family, we do things this way."
Regarding Anonymity on the Internet	1. For Safety: never give your name, address, or location to anyone on the Internet: So how to square with your kid the challenges of being anonymous and not sharing their name? Talk to them about Digital Etiquette, Digital Ethics. 2. You can't remind your kid too many times at this age that what they say on the Internet needs to be at the standard of how they would speak to someone face-to-face (or better.)
Digital Footprint	What goes on the Internet, Stays on the Internet. Be kind to your future self.
Possible Sleep Issues due to device use-	All devices live at night outside your middle graders room. Ideally they charge there and aren't easily accessible or tempting to access. Devices should go away at least 30 minutes before bed.

Situation	Possible Language/Plan
Creating Screentime Boundaries	1. Distinguish between school and recreational screen time (both should count toward the total of whatever you decide) 2. Conduct a Family Meeting where everyone suggests their ideas: no phones during dinner, or before bed. 3. Create a balance of on/off-screen activities 4. Use apps and tools to both monitor, block, and create focus time (specific apps are always changing, what is most important when choosing an app is the features you want it to have and what you are looking for it to do, not which specific app it is.) 5. Discuss why you have these boundaries and rules. Middle graders are more likely to comply if they understand why. For more on why, see the sections above (sleep, mental health/depression/ negative self-image) 6. If changes need to be made, specifically reducing screen time, make them gradually as this could be met with resistance] 7. Be a model. Lead by example. (Mastruserio, Pediatric and Adolescent Medicine 2023).
If there's pushback about screentime boundaries	1. "We created a plan together and we aren't going to change it on the spot. If we want to change it, we need to discuss it as a family and that isn't going to happen now. 2. "I can tell that you're upset with this boundary, but right now it's my job to enforce it. We made these rules together and agreed as a family." 3. "This is a complicated thing you are asking for and I cannot discuss it with you on the fly. If you'd like to discuss it together, let's make a time when we can give it the time and space it deserves" (paraphrased from Dr. BeckyGoodinside)

Situation	Possible Language/Plan
Work vs. Recreational Screen Time	1. Have a different place for recreational vs. Worktime screentime 2. Make sure they tell you when the transition happened so that you aren't counting "worktime" 3. Figure out whether work time has to come first or not otherwise they'll equivocate about it forever. 4. Figure out a focus app that they want to use. Have it be their idea somehow.
Your kid is multi-tasking	It's a myth. All the data says so.
Checking to see if a website is trustworthy	• Are there a lot of misspellings? • Are there a lot of pop-up ads? • Does it look professional? • Is it edu, org, or gov? (CommonSense Education, 2021).
Helpful ways to use AI (carefully)	• Proofreading and editing their work (if they are allowed to) the prompt has to be very specific. "Please Proofread and edit ONLY" • "I am brainstorming essay ideas for the book, To Kill a Mockingbird, what would be some good themes to start with? • "Please remove all formatting from this document" • "Please translate this into _____" • "Please help me come up with a good apology for my friend. I _____"
Your kid did something inappropriate on the Internet	• Keep a calm demeanor. • Ask what happened. • Listen" • Have them make amends/follow school's requirements for logical consequences

8

Good People Who Do Good Things

Personal Inventory

When you were in middle school, on a scale of 1–10, how concerned were you about world events?
1   2   3   4   5   6   7   8   9   10

The environment?
1   2   3   4   5   6   7   8   9   10

Were you involved in community service?

My memories of middle school are confined to the place of the school itself. The news that we concerned ourselves with circled our locker area, where the bikes were kept, and the field where we walked when we were supposed to be running the mile. We spread information about each other and didn't seem to think about the world so much. We knew we were supposed to be concerned about the ozone, and Chernobyl, but we spent a lot of time talking about ourselves.

It isn't that middle graders today are necessarily less concerned about how they look or what they are wearing or what their perceived popularity status is, it's just that they are doing all that and they are *also* quite worried about, or, at the least required to look like they are worried about, the world in a myriad of

DOI: 10.4324/9781003527831-9

different ways, trending or not. Of all the middle-grade students I've spoken to, climate change is one of the things at the top of their list of things that keep them up at night. Mental health issues, school shootings, poverty, wars – they are aware, they are concerned. They are tapped in and, as opposed to the ethos of when I was growing up in high school when we felt like we were "over it" and history had ended, most of these students instead feel an intense need to make a difference, or at least pressure to do so.

Whether it's in their communities or the world, there are models they look to, Greta and Malala, and they can see examples of people who are like them, who have been young, who have never thought for a second that there wasn't a reason to be apathetic, instead, rallying and making a difference and inspiring others in the process.

In School: Project-Based Learning and Design Thinking

Project-based learning is a learning pedagogy by which students learn through real-world and personally engaging, often collaborative projects ("What is PBL") that are tailor-made for projects that have real-world impact. Design thinking, its sister pedagogy, is a problem-based, human-based approach that starts with how to improve things for someone, to fill a need, and to iterate and create something to fill that need (IDEO, "Design Thinking"). Design thinking has active steps where students need to practice skills that they may not have facility with yet – with stakes that are higher than in a usual classroom: they need to listen, observe, research, design, create, iterate, adjust, and make something meaningful. And they care because they are making it for someone and a reason.

Examples of project-based learning are climate-change mitigation projects, like the kind our sixth graders do in their STEM class, or the entrepreneurial intervention for social change project similar to the one our eighth graders do. Both of these projects potentially have real-world impact. Students are tasked with creating an invention and marketing it to venture capitalists to see if they will invest in it. This year, students pitched a romance app for seniors to match with each other, removable pockets for clothes that don't have them, and a water filter that uses com-postable filters.

These kinds of opportunities require students to take skills across disciplines and think about how to apply the things they know to look at the world and add something to it that is new or will change or improve something that already exists. These kinds of intellectual exercises, whether or not students get VC buy-in are the point, not as much the end product. Designing a product with a user in mind, thinking about their needs, getting outside their own experience, and imaging another's perspective is not an easy task for a middle grader and it is an excellent way of helping them to not only think in a more complex way but to stretch their social and emotional abilities to look at the perspectives of their fellows so that they can extend this perspective taking to, momentarily at least, move beyond the developmentally appropriate concern of others' perceptions, to a concern about the experience of others and how to improve it.

Social Justice

Teachers are also adding social justice pedagogies to the curriculum to stretch students' abilities to think outside themselves, to broaden their understanding of human experience and history, and to hear voices and stories that are not usually part of the dominant narrative. Social justice work activates students' civic duty as well as their feelings of responsibility toward others. One very important learning lesson from social justice in classrooms is students learning that not everyone thinks like them, has the same value system as they do, or holds the same beliefs:

> That doesn't mean you can't talk about controversial issues; in fact, teaching students how to respectfully discuss an issue *with people who don't see things the same way* is a lesson that will serve them for the rest of their lives.
>
> (Gonzalez)

Middle graders are doing so much work: emotional, social, academic, and personal – but one of the best parts of working on social justice work, design thinking, or project-based learning with others at the core of the projects is that it synthesizes so many of the skills that they are learning and requires them to put together all these things. They are ready to do this work where they look outside themselves and begin to learn greater perspective and empathy. It's a stretch, but it is a stretch that is in their Zone of Proximal Development.

Activating the Better Angels of Their Natures: Looking Outside Themselves

Service Learning

Community service has been a part of education for years, but service learning, a new and improved model, combines service to the community with curricular integration, academic connections, assessment, and reflection similar to what is seen in project-based learning as we discussed in the previous section (Wolpert, "Service Learning").

Studies have shown that it helps to improve drop-out rates for students who are struggling academically or who are at risk (Bridgeland et al.). And, as motivation is a challenge for some students at this stage, making meaning needs to be primary – some students just need stakes to make things matter to them. Making meaning is the neurological goal of the gray matter rearrangement and pruning of the synapses and neurons, of the reticular activating system and hippocampus that decide what is important to remember long term and what can be gotten rid of. Whether it is building a structure for someone that will last and be used or making sure that water in the taps at their school has levels of chlorine that are safe to drink, there are always some students who *must* feel like there is a reason, a why, beyond compliance, beyond grades – and for those students who are motivated by caring for others, this can be a ticket into a larger world of meaning, and one of rich interdisciplinary synthesis and community impact (Robinson).

The cross-disciplinary impact is a primary reason to do this kind of work, as well as how middle school students themselves are the active learners and the shapers of the learning experience:

At the heart of middle school philosophy is a belief that the organization of the curriculum should transcend separate subject areas. One of the primary curriculum organizers for accomplishing this goal suggests focusing on themes that emerge from the concerns of middle school students themselves. Through service learning experiences, schooling is linked to issues and questions of significance to students. Students learn to ask questions and devise answers to the questions.

(Schukar)

And for all students, this stretches their prefrontal cortex and works their empathy muscles.

Indeed, a study by Rebecca Robinson on Adolescent brains found that:

Students expressed greater emotional responses following a service learning experience and explained that the emotional response was an indication of greater engagement in the learning experience. This benefit may be even more pronounced in younger adolescents as their brains show increased activity in emotional regions ... This approach helps students to connect their learning to their sense of self and who they want to be.

(Robinson)

Community Service

It can be challenging for middle graders to do community service, even with their schools. Many non-profits prefer high school-age students or begin taking students to volunteer at age 13.

Have a conversation together as a family about the causes that matter to you. If there is consensus, fantastic, look for opportunities to volunteer or other ways to support that cause. Often raising money is a way for students to put others before themselves, identify a goal, and figure out ways to reach it through leadership and ingenuity, not to mention empathy and care for others.

If there isn't consensus, choose a place or cause per month and take turns going to support it. Whether it's a food bank, or picking up trash along the beach, doing this kind of work as a family will help your middle graders to know your family values, and it will help them to look outside their experiences and see that they can make a difference, even now – while they are still in middle school.

Ethics: Practicing for Life

It's easy to say "Do the right thing," but in real life, situations are rarely ever so cut and dry.

Growing up, children are exposed to cartoons and media where there is a good guy and a bad guy, and, without ever interrogating that schema, they can apply it to every situation they encounter as they age, too – in the middle grades, in high school, in college, and as an adult. But it would be better, for them, for their communities, and for the world, if they were able to take a softer, more nuanced view of the world. A view in which there is an infusion of empathy, perspective, and an imperative to look at a situation from multiple angles no matter how uncomfortable it makes them feel.

By this point you KNOW that this already is not in a middle-grader bailiwick, but good news! Arguing is, or, if you want to be less pugilistic about it, "debating" is. Ethical dilemmas are a great way to engage middle-grade students with questions of ethics, empathy, and the idea that there might NOT be one right way of looking at a situation, and that there are situations in which there are gray zones.

Giving students a chance to flex and develop ethical musculature will help them to be able to exercise it later when the stakes are higher and when they are called upon to weigh in on something when more is in the balance. As anything, it's a skill. If you haven't practiced looking at how to think about ethics, this will be a challenging thing to do quickly. Which is usually how a real-life ethical dilemma unfolds.

A good place to start is whether they think that people are inherently good or whether they need to be taught to be good people.

Mengzi, or Mencius, who lived in the fourth century BCE, had the theory that human beings were inherently good. He based this on his theory that in a scenario in which a child was about to fall into a well, a person's body, soul, and mind would immediately be activated to go do something about it – whether the person DOES do anything is immaterial to the scenario, it's just that initial impulse that's important (Mencius). This is a good conversation to have with middle graders – and one that will produce many options – do they agree with Mencius? Why or why not? If humans are inherently good do they need to learn how to be good? Or do we need to do something else entirely? What does it mean to be good? Does it change for different settings and different people?

In terms of that last question is also Kohlberg's Stages of Moral Development to consider, to have them ponder that depending on circumstances, there may not be a simple cut-and-dry "right thing" to do in a situation. Similar to Jean Valjean and his loaf of bread to save his starving sister's child in *Les Misérables*, Lawrence Kohlberg posits a scenario about a man, Heinz, who ultimately steals medication from a chemist's laboratory for his wife because he can't afford it and if she doesn't get it she will die:

Heinz's wife was dying from a particular type of cancer. Doctors said a new drug might save her. The drug had been discovered by a local chemist, and the Heinz tried desperately to buy some, but the chemist was charging ten times the money it cost to make the drug, and this was much more than the Heinz could afford:

> Heinz could only raise half the money, even after help from family and friends. He explained to the chemist that his wife was dying and asked if he could have the drug cheaper or pay the rest of the money later. The chemist refused, saying that he had discovered the drug and was going to make money from it. The husband was desperate to save his wife, so later that night he broke into the chemist's and stole the drug.
>
> Should Heinz have broken into the laboratory to steal the drug for his wife? Why or why not?
>
> (Mcleod, "Kohlberg")

Kolhberg gave this ethical dilemma to several students and categorized their answers. Some students said that breaking the law is breaking the law no matter what. Some students said that the wife's life is more important than the law and so Heinz stealing the medicine was justified by any terms necessary.

Kohlberg's Stages of Moral Development

LEVEL	STAGE	DEFINITION	RESPONSE TO HEINZ DILEMMA
Preconventional	1. Avoiding Punishment	Moral reasoning is based on direct consequences.	Heinz should not steal the drug because stealing is illegal, and he could be punished.
	2. Self-Interest	Actions are seen in terms of rewards rather than moral value.	Heinz should not steal the drug because stealing is illegal, and he could be punished.
Conventional	3. Good boy attitude	Good behavior is about living up to social expectations and roles.	Heinz should steal the drug because, as a good husband, he is expected to do whatever he can to save his wife.
	4. Law & Order Morality	Moral reasoning considers societal laws.	Heinz should not steal the drug because he must uphold the law and maintain societal order.
Postconventional	5. Social Contract	Rules are seen as social agreements that can be changed when necessary.	Heinz should steal the drug because preserving human life is a more fundamental value than property rights.
	6. Universal Principles	Moral reasoning is based on universal ethical principles and justice.	Heinz should consider non-violent civil disobedience or negotiation with the pharmacist. The decision reflects a conflict between property rights and the sanctity of human life.

While it isn't necessarily useful or necessary to put students' thinking in this exact framework, Kohlberg's schema speaks to gray areas of ethics and morality. For students who are just starting to flex their muscles in this area, it is good practice to do this. And you can watch them as they change their opinions over time.

Ethical questions rarely have a correct answer.

One type of question we often give students asks them to think about the tension between family and self or community and self as these are challenges that are relevant to them.

For example: Leila is a singer and would like to pursue opera when she grows up. She has a really important performance on the same night as her family's Eid celebration. Should she go to the Eid celebration or should she go to the performance? You might think at first blush that students would look at it from their perspective, but the first thing they often do is try to bend the circumstances so that the situation is different. It's a common and interesting tactic. Good for future community organizers! They will, rightly so, question why a performance is being held on Eid and say that that should change. Not wrong.

But then they look at the question from all angles, from the perspective of her family, from her community – both those she might be performing with as well as her religious community. Often you can't predict how the students will land. They end up talking about topics that are very relevant and personal to them. These kinds of conversations can bring them to a place of deeper empathy with each other, not just with the hypothetical person experiencing the ethical dilemma. For example, when we were studying a question similar to this, I had a student say, "Both my parents are immigrants and they have sacrificed too much for me. No matter what, I would always do the thing that respected them the most."

These students will grow up to be the next crop of leaders, voters, business owners, artists, parents, teachers, doctors, lawyers, programmers, scientists, writers, and thinkers – we want them to be able to think through things. We don't always have to agree, but if they've truly thought something through and have examined it from multiple perspectives, we can feel assured that they are growing in ethical responsibility to handle what comes next from a moral perspective.

Our students can act with justice and ethics in mind, and think first of others. They can see the world in nuance. They can know that only in stories is there one bad guy and one good guy – that in life situations require deeper analysis, and that through examinations of ethics, they will have the skills to do that work.

Ethics: Practicing NOW
The good news for students is that they don't need to wait to do the right thing. There are so many different opportunities that

will come up for middle-grade students to have a chance to do the right thing. Don't get me wrong, no matter how naturally nice and kind they are, and/or no matter how much work they've done to build up their ethical skills, they will still slip and make mistakes. This is an age where impulse sometimes rules the moment. Perfection isn't the goal. But practice absolutely is. There are so many opportunities in middle school to practice saying the ethical thing, thinking through what the ethical thing is, and then doing the ethical thing.

The biggest thing you can do to support your student in ethical behavior toward others is to model it yourself. Each time your student talks about their friend or, even more importantly, *not* their friend, you can help them to do better. "I wonder" sentences are good:

"I wonder why so-and-so made that choice. Do you have any ideas?"

"I wonder if they are feeling lonely?" What do you think?

"I wonder if there is a way of looking at that that makes their actions make more sense."

"I wonder if we can figure out a way of thinking through this situation in a way that helps you feel less icky about your choices."

"I wonder if they have something going on that we aren't aware of."

All of these things, whether they end up being rhetorical or not, can help your middle grader to pause before immediately judging their peers and will help them develop their empathy muscles.

There are also the action ethical choices, which are great to discuss through film, books, TV shows, and real-life examples. You just have to *use* the examples:

"Do you think that so-and-so was right to do that to her sister? Even though her sister did it first?"

"I wonder why so-and-so made that choice to go see the Grateful Dead over the summer instead of join the Mathletes. Why do you think?"

The conversations are what's important: looking at things from multiple angles, thinking about others' perspectives, and getting a handle on multiple ways to see the world, including a better handle on how they themselves see the world. Practicing now is also practicing for the future.

Taking Care of Others

Jobs

Some small and very important ways to help students continue to look outside themselves and increase their ability for empathy are jobs – specifically jobs around their homes, and jobs where they help others. Not necessarily "jobs" as in earning money, though that can be part of it, but jobs as in they *work*.

Taking Care of Space

One is chores around their own living spaces.

Every place is its ecosystem. Whether it's one room or multiple rooms, some tasks need to be done repeatedly, over and over, to keep things running. Housework is a repetitive process and can either be onerous, or a habit, or perhaps both.

Chores are another important time when middle graders and grown-ups need to have a conversation about expectations. If your middle graders don't know the expectations, the explicit and very, very clear expectations you have of them, they will not be able to fulfill those expectations. I say this because sometimes, as our kids get bigger and more capable – capable of doing *really* impressive things, we assume that they know what we expect them to do, and if they don't do them, we create a narrative of deficit that may or may not have anything to do with the reality of your middle grader's intention. For example. Perhaps I expected my middle grader to put their plate in the sink when they were finished eating. But I expected it and never told them that. Maybe I think to myself, "I shouldn't HAVE to tell them that. They should just KNOW." But that's not how the middle-grade brain, nay, the human brain, works.

So have a meeting. Make a list of all the chores. If you want to make it fancy, put all the chores on cards or popsicle sticks. Have your middle grader pick out the cards that they are going to do every day for this month and two extra bonuses they will do during the week at some point.

Now is when you might start thinking about allowances and money. Honestly, I don't have one answer for that. I don't love the idea of making their part of the house cleaning connected with money. My kids know that they get no money for the baseline chores that they are required to do. However, if they'd like to earn money, there are plenty of other cards for the taking.

That's how I've gotten around the allowance issue. No allowance, per se, but they can earn money by doing extra work around the house.

Taking Care

Another opportunity that presented itself in my house for my older sons to earn money was unique to our family but bears mentioning because the situation may have some takeaways for the larger conversation.

The youngest of the three kids has a double diagnosis of cystic fibrosis, a genetic disease that affects the lungs, digestive system, and pancreas, and type 1 diabetes, which, at times, can be stressful and upsetting for everyone in the house. He manages like aces – he's got a great attitude, and we've tried very hard to make it so his brothers, the current middle graders of the family, get what they need in terms of attention, of course. The youngest needs to do two breathing treatments a day with his shaky vest and we were struggling, between our jobs and the three kids, to fit them in between school, extracurriculars, and bedtime, so we engaged the older boys. We paid them, not much, but not nothing, per breathing treatment, and they learned how to do them and we never missed one while we had that system going. I share this because there are always opportunities for kids to step up and take responsibility, especially in unique circumstances. Now they might *have* to. It might not be a choice. It's hard on a kid to take too much responsibility, so if they are stretched, be their grown-up in another way so that they can take off somewhere.

Many kids are not in that position. They don't have to stretch in that way, and so helping someone who has a medical condition, helping an elderly neighbor, babysitting, or tutoring a younger sibling or cousin are great ways for a middle grader to take on mentorship roles where they can feel that sense of responsibility. It is a feeling of strength and importance. A powerful rush that can ameliorate feelings of powerlessness that can crop up in a middle-grade setting.

There is nothing like that feeling of taking care of someone else who needs you. I mean, after all, we know that quite well.

Talk Middle Grader to Me: Chapter 8

Situation	Possible Language
Modeling Giving Benefit of the Doubt: I wonder questions	" I wonder why so and so made that choice. Do you have any ideas?" "I wonder if they are feeling lonely?" What do you think? "I wonder if there is a way of looking at that that makes their actions make more sense." "I wonder if we can figure out a way of thinking through this situation in a way that helps you feel less icky about your choices." "I wonder if they have something going on that we aren't aware of."
Using TV and books, and movies as examples to reflect on	"Do you think that so and so was right to do that to her sister? Even though her sister did it first?" "I wonder why so and so made that choice to go see the Grateful Dead over the summer instead of join the Mathletes" Why do you think?"

Conclusion: From Chaos to Context

Everybody rides the carousel, and no one knows where they get on and where they get off. We are all doing our best here. When I started my job as a middle school division director, the first thing I did was hang this carousel painting my father made in my office. That carousel always reminds me to remember that everyone is in some stage of development. It doesn't have to be one of the ones laid out by Erikson – and it doesn't have to be according to any particular theory or book. We are all riding our own rides here. We get to choose the color of our horses, maybe, but we really don't get much of a say whether we are on one of those horses that goes up really high and down really low super fast, or

DOI: 10.4324/9781003527831-10

one that goes at a more leisurely pace. We don't really know till we've ridden whatever ride we are on for a while. We learn while we ride, and we can share what we learn with our middle graders – and if there's anyone on those horses that is going at full tilt, it's them. We can support them by being by their side, helping them to remember that it's a ride, it'll be over, and then they can choose a different horse, maybe one that will be a bit chiller. And they'll have better tools.

But everyone rides the carousel.

I remember it every time I see my dad's orange woodcut there on my wall. I want you to remember it too.

The goal of this book, from the beginning to the end, is to give every middle grader's parent/guardian/adult/grown-up the ability to take a load off and allow part of the process, not all of the process, but parts of the process to unfold.

It's hard to be a parent right now. We didn't expect this when we were thinking about raising children – that our main challenges would be all of how puberty and brain development would influence how our children would push back on the screen time boundaries that we set. Or that we would be so torn because their screen time is just SO social or that so much of their schooling would require them to be online, or that it would feel so much like we needed to be doing something but we weren't quite sure what it was.

But we do know, is that if we *don't* do it – whatever "it" is, or if we didn't do something in the past, our kid might not turn out OK, certainly they won't get into college or get a job or be happy and successful. Of course, this is hyperbole, but tell the truth, doesn't it feel like this sometimes? That if you mess up, it's just going to fall apart?

And on top of all of this, you are the grown-up for a kid who is going THROUGH it.

Middle graders go through so much in such a short long time. We should give them some kind of medal when they're done. The amount of growing that their brain does, their body does – the academic leaps, the emotional depth that they can eventually get to by eighth grade (fingers crossed).

The goal of this book is to support *you*, the grown-up of the middle grader, to help them to make what sometimes feels like pure chaos contextualized so that they can understand *themselves* better.

So that *you* can also understand them better.

Imagine a string of tangled white fairy lights. When you started this book, if you came at it with the concept of the middle-grade years being that string of tangled fairy lights, now as you are finishing, now that you have thought about your own experiences of being a middle grader, raising/parenting a middle grader or anticipating raising/parenting a middle grader, now that you've untangled some of the assumptions you had and contextualized them as normal developments of the body and brain and seen that being a parent of a middle grader doesn't mean you necessarily need to do MORE, in fact, realized sometimes you need to do *less* in order for your middle grader to take up the part that they need to – now that you've done all that, the chaos will be calmer, smoothed, contextualized. You are receptive, calm, and consistent.

The idea is that *now*, most, at least, of these strings of fairy lights have untangled as a result of all these understandings, and, because of this, the lights are all now turned on and sparkling around the room so that you can enjoy the experience of *being* with your middle grader. An experience that can (sometimes) be enjoyable.

That was the goal of this book.

Because this time is too important, the time that our kids are with us is too short to be years of *actual* chaos. It needs to be a time of connection, of understanding. These years can be the foundation for trust going forward: when your middle grader feels like you see and hear them. These are years for you to be the constant while their world feels chaotic. They will see that you are *trying* to see and hear them, even though, you, as a human, make mistakes. Which they appreciate because it allows them to be human too.

This time is vital. No pressure. But not just because it's four years, but because it's four years before the *next* four years of high school when the stakes are higher. But it's vital in all the best ways.

Sometimes the best ways to parent middle graders is to breathe, let things unfold, and just be there. Receptive. Consistent. Calm.

One of the BEST parts about middle school is the messiness. Everyone gets to make mistakes. You get to tangle those fairy lights up and untangle them again. Which is harder to do in high school.

You want those habits, of listening, and asking if they want you to just listen, or if they want you to problem-solve, meeting together and setting expectations, talking through logical consequences when necessary, and having conversations about drugs, alcohol, and sex. You want your middle grader, once they are a high schooler, to keep coming to you. Because in high school things will inevitably get more real.

Be Receptive, Calm, and Consistent. Be that when they are in middle school and you'll be that when they are in high school.

You'll be that, more or less consistently, the whole time, through college and beyond.

You aren't going to get the right balance right away. Balancing requires continued movement of your arms to steady you to make sure that you are not leaning too far one way or the other.

So practice, practice balancing.

There's no time like the present.

Additional Resources

Books

- *How to Talk So Kids Will Listen & Listen So Kids Will Talk* by Adele Faber and Elaine Mazlish
- *Congrats! You're Having a Teen: Strengthen Your Family and Raise a Good Person* by Dr. Kenneth R. Ginsberg
- *Middle School Makeover: Improving the Way You and Your Child Experience the Middle School Years* by Michelle Icard
- *Untangled: Guiding Teenage Girls Through the Seven Transitions into Adulthood* by Lisa Damour
- *The Emotional Lives of Teenagers: Raising Connected, Capable, and Compassionate Adolescents* by Lisa Damour
- *Raising Confident Black Kids: A Comprehensive Guide for Empowering Parents and Teachers of Black Children* by M.J. Fievre
- *Growing Up in Public: Coming of Age in a Digital World* by Devorah Heitner
- *This is so Awkward: Modern Puberty Explained* by Cara Natterson, MD and Vanessa Kroll Bennett
- *Queen Bees and Wannabees* by Rosalind Wiseman
- *The Anxious Generation: How the Great Rewiring of Childhood Is Causing an Epidemic of Mental Illness* by Jonathan Haidt – supplements for each chapter

Websites and Online Communities

- Parenting.com: a comprehensive site offering articles, advice, and resources for all stages of parenting.
- Common Sense Media: provides reviews and advice on media, technology, and digital citizenship for children.

- ◆ Understood.org: offers resources for parents of children with learning and attention issues.
- ◆ ADDitude Magazine: a resource for parents of children with ADHD and other learning differences.
- ◆ Cult of Pedagogy: for educators, but a great resource to contextualize these years.

Research Articles and Journals

- ◆ *Journal of Early Adolescence*: academic journal focusing on research related to early adolescence.
- ◆ *Child Development Journal*: offers peer-reviewed research on the development of children.
- ◆ *Educational Leadership*: provides articles on educational practices and policies, including those relevant to middle school education.

Professional Organizations

- ◆ National PTA (Parent-Teacher Association): offers resources and support for parents involved in their children's education.
- ◆ American Academy of Pediatrics (AAP): guides child health and development.

Podcasts

- ◆ The Puberty Podcast
- ◆ Ask Lisa: The Psychology of Parenting

Discussion Questions

Introduction

1. The author suggests that they may be imperfect in their parenting. Given this, it raises the question of the validity and potential ramifications of offering parenting advice while facing parenting challenges. What are your thoughts on this tension? *Is* there a tension?
2. The author talks about "playing the long game" in terms of parenting. Do you see parenting as "playing the long game" or does another analogy work better?
3. The author says that children of this age are both "predictable" and "unique." Are these contradictory? Why or why not? Do you agree or disagree?

Chapter 1: Spoiler Alert: It's Puberty. Puberty's the Problem

1. The author starts each chapter with a "Personal Inventory." Is it necessary to revisit one's own experiences to be able to effectively support your child's experiences in middle school? Why or why not?
2. Mircea Eliade says a liminal stage is when something is not quite one thing and not quite the other. How does puberty work in this construct and what makes liminal stages challenging? What are benefits to liminal stages?
3. Have you been surprised at your child's physical or emotional changes during puberty? How have you reacted?
4. What kinds of conversations have you had with your middle grader around puberty? How have they been received? Do you have tips to share with others?
5. What kind of hygiene conversations have you needed to have so far? What do you *wish* you could say? What do you think your middle grader wishes they could say?

6. Does your child upsize or downsize their issues? What about you? What are the strategies you use to help right-size things?

Middle Grader and Grown-Up Discussion Section Chapter 1
Pick **two** to discuss (at a time):

1. Why do you think puberty happens at this time? Do you think it should happen earlier or later? Would things be easier or more challenging?
2. Share something you wish your grown-up knew about your experience of puberty so far (not *necessarily* the nitty-gritty stuff!). Share something you wish your *middle grader* knew about how you are experiencing THEIR puberty experience so far.
3. What is/was your experience with hygiene products? What do you wish you had? What do you wish you didn't have to use? Is there something you'd stop or start doing in terms of taking care of your hygiene or how you look if it didn't matter what other people thought?
4. How often do you worry about what other people think about how you look? How often do YOU worry about how you look?
5. Is there a part of your body that you're worried about specifically? Share if you would like to talk about it.
6. How comfortable are you talking about gender and sex? Would you be able to talk about something important? Why or why not? How can we help make sure to get you to a place you feel more comfortable?
7. What are ways we can tell if something is a big deal or a small deal?
8. What are the criteria for going to an adult if there's a problem? How do you know if it's an emergency or a THING?

Chapter 2: Unveiling the Adolescent Brain

1. How much do you know about your own brain? Do you remember when you became conscious? When did things "click" for you?

2. The author discusses the need for "Brain Ed" along with Puberty Ed. Do you agree or disagree? Why or why not?

3. Does knowing that middle graders often appear more mature than their brains' actual developmental stage change the way you perceive them? Why or why not?

4. The author makes a clear statement that there are some decisions that are too much responsibility developmentally for a middle grader to make at this age. Is this something that your experience bears out, or have you experienced something different?

5. How comfortable are you discussing risky behaviors (sex, drugs, etc.) with your middle grader? What steps might you need to take to get more comfortable?

6. Are creating firm boundaries something you struggle with or something that you struggle to bend when necessary? Knowing which you are is important!

7. Do you feel like you can step in when necessary and talk to other grown-ups when there has been a break in the community of middle schoolers? What about helping your middle grader to advocate for themselves? How can you get more comfortable with taking these steps?

Middle Grader and Grown-Up Discussion Section Chapter 2

Pick **two** to discuss (at a time):

1. How can we use knowledge about the brain to help during middle school?

2. What strategies will be helpful for me/you during an amygdala hijack? When do they happen most often? Where can I go that is safe/relatively private to chill if it happens at school?

3. Does knowing that my reactive brain is just trying to save me from being eaten by a bear help me appreciate it when it's hijacking my body's reactions? Why or why not? Does it help me to regulate again?

4. Do you ever worry/did you ever worry that you weren't as "good" as your peers at a particular subject or skill? Did you ever think about the fact that it might just be because you're on a different timeline and you might be as good, if not better in the future? Why or why not?

5. Do you think that you are capable of improvement in skills and talents or do you think you're "just good at things and that's it"? How does that affect how you do things in middle school?

6. Do you know that everyone feels bad about themselves and worries about how smart they are or how good at things they are or whether people like them or whether they are a good person – even if it looks like everything is going well for them? It's true. Do you believe that? Why or why not?

7. What do you know about the importance of sleep at your age? What do you DO? What's the difference? Why?

8. Have you ever said something mean about someone else for no reason? Why? Did you feel bad about it later? Why do you think people do that in middle school?

Chapter 3: It's Time for Identity Exploration

1. Do you hope your child goes into a career in something they are passionate about or something practical?

2. What is something that you currently do that gets you out of your comfort zone and into your Zone of Proximal Development?

3. The author says "you get the kid you get." Do you agree or disagree? Why or why not?

4. Are you worried about your child being over- or under-scheduled? Who is creating the pressure and worry?

5. Does your child mostly enjoy their extracurriculars?

6. Is your child experiencing an equity gap in the realm of extra-curriculars? Let's brainstorm together how to ameliorate this: contact @chaostocontext.

Middle Grader and Grown-Up Discussion Section Chapter 3
Pick **two** to discuss (at a time):

1. Which extracurriculars do you enjoy doing? Which do you wish you could do? Which do you wish you didn't have to do?

2. Do you feel like you are learning more about what kind of person you are? Are you ever surprised at what you discover about yourself?
3. How are you different from when you were in elementary school? What changes have you noticed? Why do you think you've changed?
4. Do you ever feel like the grown-ups around you wish you were someone else or that you were like someone else? Was there anything specific that caused you to feel that way?
5. What do you think your grown-ups wish you would do when you grow up?
6. What do you think your grown-ups wished they would do when they grew up when they were your age?

Chapter 4: The Changing Social Dynamics of Middle School

1. The author presents a theory of friendship that posits that affinity groups, perceived coolness factor, and proximity are the main reasons middle graders become friends. Do you agree? Why or why not?
2. The author explains that in her experience, friendships are fluid in the middle grades. Was this your experience growing up? Is this your middle grader's experience? Discuss.
3. How can the personal fable and imaginary audience be used for good in the middle grades? Can they?
4. Do you agree with the author that conflict can be good? Why or why not?
5. The difference between respect, as earned, and dignity, as given as virtue of being a person, is one that can help in a middle-grade classroom. Do you see any other contexts in which this construct could be useful?
6. Does your middle grader also think that you "vacuum weird"? What does vacuuming weird even mean? Discuss.

Middle Grader and Grown-Up Discussion Section Chapter 4

Pick **two** to discuss (at a time):

1. Do you feel like your friends are sometimes your friends and sometimes not? Do you ever feel like you aren't sure where you stand? How does that feel?
2. Have you ever had the feeling that you are in a movie or onstage or that you're being watched in some way? When do you feel like this? Why do you think this happens?
3. How do you feel about mistakes? How do you feel when you make them? How does it feel in your body? What do you DO? How do you fix them?
4. When you make a mistake with a friend? What are the steps you take? How can you make sure that you don't make the same mistake again?
5. Do you know when to get an adult if a friend shares something that makes you think they might be in trouble?
6. Have you ever been the one who was mean? How did that feel? How did you make amends?

Chapter 5: The Roles of Grown-Ups in the Middle Grades

1. The author makes the statement that "it's hard being a parent" and "harder than it was." Do you agree? Why or why not? Has that been your experience?
2. The author identifies four reasons that it seems like parenting is a challenge. Do you relate to these?

   Fire Hose: Competing information on the Internet.
   ALL Prevention, ALL the Time: The idea that if something happens it is both preventable *and* our fault.
   Total Success Principle: Every possible thing, depending on your personal value system (academics, material wealth, network, social status, etc.) should be provided for children.
   Tummy Time for All Ages: Be involved with them all the time. What other reasons would you give?

3. The author gives the acronym: RCC, Receptive, Calm, Consistent, as characteristics to keep the relationship strong during the middle school years. Is there an acronym that suits your style better?

4. Some schools of thought feel like middle graders naturally start pulling away from their parents and going toward their peers at this time and others feel like this is detrimental to their development and that parents should have the most influence regardless. What are your thoughts? What are your wishes?

5. What do you wish you could say to your middle grader if they would listen and hear you?

6. The author lays out a number of situations and topics that might come up in the middle-grade years. What situations and topics are missing? What would you like to see? Reach out to @chaostocontext with ideas for topics or what you would want to see covered.

Middle Grader and Grown-Up Discussion Section Chapter 5

Pick **two** to discuss (at a time):

1. How much time do you like to spend with family/grown-ups in general? What feels right for you? How can we come up with a compromise that's good for everyone?

2. When and where is the best place to have a conversation?

3. What do you know about fentanyl? Let's have a discussion about it.

4. What do you wish were different about your conversations with the grown-ups around you?

5. What are things you want to learn from your grown-ups?

6. What do you want your grown-ups to learn from you?

7. If your grown-up could know anything about you what should they know to REALLY understand you?

Chapter 6: Academics and Middle School: A New Frontier

1. The author asserts that middle school is challenging because each student is at a different stage of intellectual development. Has this been a challenge for your student? Discuss.

2. The author lays out a number of configurations for middle grades in the personal inventory corner: What do you think the ideal configuration for the middle grades is? 6–8? 5–8? TK–8? TK–12? Other?

3. How has your child's unique learning needs manifested in middle school? What would you tell another parent with a child with a similar learning profile as they are entering middle school?

4. In what ways do you struggle with organization/time management/or other executive functioning skills? How does this perhaps affect your ability to support your student?

5. Often parents supporting their student's school work and EF can be challenging. What are some workarounds that you can come up with so that you can maintain a positive relationship with your middle grader?

Middle Grader and Grown-Up Discussion Section Chapter 6

Pick **two** to discuss (at a time):

1. How has starting middle school been for you? Have the academics been challenging or feeling OK? What would you change if you could wave a magic wand? *Would* you change something?

2. How do you organize things? Do you like to work in a clean space or do you prefer your space to have your things in your own way? Describe your ideal workspace.

3. What are ways that your grown-up can support you with your homework, organization work, or time management in a way that will be helpful to you?

4. How do you feel about advocating for yourself to your teachers? How can your grown-ups help you?

5. Do you have a learning difference or another challenge? What skills do you have that other people don't have because of this difference?

6. Would you drink water out of a fish tank? Don't. Don't drink water out of a fish tank.

Chapter 7: Our Collective Challenge: Technology, Social Media, and the Middle Grades

1. What kinds of challenges are you having with technology and your middle grader already?
2. Do you allow your child to have a phone? Social media? Why or why not? If not, what is your reasoning? If yes, what is your reasoning?
3. Has the pandemic shaped the way you view technology and your children? If so, in what ways?
4. What types of screen time limitations are currently in place at home? How often are you able to adhere to the rules you put in place? What are the main barriers that prevent you from being able to follow through?
5. Some families have taken screens out of their homes completely. Have you done this? How did it go? Would you do this if it was possible? Why or why not? What would it look like if you did? How would your lives be different? What would your children miss out on? What would they be able to do?
6. Are you comfortable texting another parent about something mean/violent/inappropriate their child said in a chat? Would you want a parent to share that kind of information with you?
7. How much information about digital citizenship do you think your child has? Do you think they are able to exercise the knowledge they have?
8. Do you wish your child spent less time on screens? How much less? If so, what small steps could you take to make that a reality?

Middle Grader and Grown-Up Discussion Section Chapter 7
Pick **two** to discuss (at a time):

1. Fill in the blank: "What goes on the Internet ____ _____ _____ _____."
2. In terms of technology, what do you think is a good amount of time to be on screens in a day?

3. Do you wish you were on screens more or less?
4. Do you think grown-ups worry too much about screens or not enough? Do you think middle schoolers don't worry about screens enough or too much?
5. At what age do you think social media should be available for kids? Why?
6. How many of your friends have a phone?
7. What do you wish were different about technology? Why?

Chapter 8: Good People Who Do Good Things

1. The author makes a case that social justice learning expands perspectives in middle grades. Is there ever a time when this is too much for this age group?
2. The author makes a distinction between community service and service learning. How important is it to you that your middle grader learns these skills? Why?
3. The author shares that ethical dilemmas are a good way to stretch middle grader's ethical muscles. How will I feel if my middle grader expresses views I disagree with? How will I handle it?
4. What kind of chores do you have your middle grader do?
5. Does your middle grader have particular challenges at home that give them increased responsibility? How do you think this affects their growth and development?

Middle Grader and Grown-Up Discussion Section Chapter 8
Pick **two** to discuss (at a time):

1. What chores do you think you could do that you aren't doing?
2. Say a little about the amount of responsibilities you feel you take on at home. Do you feel like they are too much? Too little?
3. What do you learn at school about social justice? How would you define social justice? What is your idea of "justice"?
4. What do you think it means to be ethical? Why are ethics important?

5. What are ways to handle differences in opinion with you and your family? How do you feel about that?
6. What does it mean to be responsible?
7. How will I know if I am a good person?

References

Introduction

Ross, Elizabeth. "The Critical Link between Parent and Teen Mental Health." *Harvard Graduate School of Education*, www.gse.harvard.edu/ideas/usable-knowledge/23/08/understanding-relationship-between-parent-and-teen-mental-health#:~:text=According%20to%20the%20study%2C%20"depressed,to%20have%20an%20anxious%20parent. Accessed 27 Apr. 2024.

Chapter 1: Spoiler Alert: It's Puberty. Puberty's the Problem

"APA Dictionary of Psychology." *American Psychological Association*, dictionary.apa.org/latency-stage. Accessed 24 Apr. 2024.

Arky, Beth. "Why Are Kids Different at Home and at School?" *Child Mind Institute*, 6 Nov. 2023, childmind.org/article/kids-different-home-school/.

Austin, A. et al. "Suicidality among Transgender Youth: Elucidating the Role of Interpersonal Risk Factors." *Journal of Interpersonal Violence*, U.S. National Library of Medicine, pubmed.ncbi.nlm.nih.gov/32345113/. Accessed 24 Apr. 2024

Breehl, Logen. "Physiology, Puberty." *StatPearls* [Internet], U.S. National Library of Medicine, 27 Mar. 2023, www.ncbi.nlm.nih.gov/books/NBK534827/#:~:text=Puberty%20is%20associated%20with%20emotional,onset%20of%20menstruation%20(menarche).

Damour, Lisa . *The Emotional Lives of Teenagers: Raising Connected, Capable, and Compassionate Adolescents*. Random House Publishing Group. Kindle Edition, p. 70.

De Rosa, C. J. et al. "Sexual Intercourse and Oral Sex among Public Middle School Students: Prevalence and Correlates." *Perspectives on Sexual and Reproductive Health*, U.S. National Library of Medicine, pubmed.ncbi.nlm.nih.gov/20887288/#:~:text=Results%3A%20Overall%2C%209%25%20of,43%25%20had%20had%20multiple%20partners. Accessed 24 Apr. 2024.

Emmanuel, Mickey, and Brooke Bokor. "Tanner Stages." *StatPearls [Internet]*, U.S. National Library of Medicine, 11 Dec. 2022, www.ncbi.nlm.nih.gov/books/NBK470280/.

"Exploring the Effect of Social Media on Teen Girls' Mental Health." *News*, 19 Apr. 2024, www.hsph.harvard.edu/news/hsph-in-the-news/exploring-the-effect-of-social-media-on-teen-girls-mental-health/.

Ginsburg, Kenneth R. *Congrats – You're Having a Teen!: Strengthen Your Family and Raise a Good Person.* American Academy of Pediatrics, 2023.

Natterson, Cara, and Vanessa Kroll Bennett. *This Is So Awkward: Modern Puberty Explained.* Harmony/Rodale. Kindle Edition, p. 91.

Reese, Jasmine. "What Is a Growth Spurt during Puberty?" *Johns Hopkins Medicine*, 8 Dec. 2023, www.hopkinsmedicine.org/health/wellness-and-prevention/what-is-a-growth-spurt-during-puberty.

Rice, E. et al. "Sexting and Sexual Behavior among Middle School Students." *Pediatrics*, U.S. National Library of Medicine, pubmed.ncbi.nlm.nih.gov/24982103/#:~:text=Students%20who%20text%20at%20least,likely%20to%20report%20sexual%20activity. Accessed 24 Apr. 2024.

"Sexual Orientation and Gender Diversity." *American Psychological Association*, www.apa.org/topics/lgbtq. Accessed 15 June 2024.

"Sexual Orientation and Gender Identity Definitions." *Human Rights Campaign*, www.hrc.org/resources/sexual-orientation-and-gender-identity-terminology-and-definitions. Accessed 24 Apr. 2024.

Zamponi, Virginia et al. "Effect of Sex Hormones on Human Voice Physiology: From Childhood to Senescence." *Hormones* (Athens, Greece), U.S. National Library of Medicine, Dec. 2021, www.ncbi.nlm.nih.gov/pmc/articles/PMC8594207/.

Chapter 2: Unveiling the Adolescent Brain

"The Adolescent Brain: Beyond Raging Hormones." *Harvard Health*, 7 Mar. 2011, www.health.harvard.edu/mind-and-mood/the-adolescent-brain-beyond-raging-hormones.

Arain, Mariam et al. "Maturation of the Adolescent Brain." *Neuropsychiatric Disease and Treatment*, U.S. National Library of Medicine, 2013, www.ncbi.nlm.nih.gov/pmc/articles/PMC3621648/.

Arguinchona, Joseph H. "Neuroanatomy, Reticular Activating System." *StatPearls [Internet]*, U.S. National Library of Medicine, 24 July 2023, www.ncbi.nlm.nih.gov/books/NBK549835/.

Armstrong, Kim. "Carol Dweck on How Growth Mindsets Can Bear Fruit in the Classroom." *Association for Psychological Science – APS*, 29 Oct. 2019, www.psychologicalscience.org/observer/dweck-growth -mindsets.

Damour, Lisa. *The Emotional Lives of Teenagers: Raising Connected, Capable, and Compassionate Adolescents*. Random House Publishing Group. Kindle Edition, p. 77.

Haber, Suzanne N. "Neuroanatomy of Reward: A View from the Ventral Striatum." *Neurobiology of Sensation and Reward*, U.S. National Library of Medicine, 1 Jan. 1970, www.ncbi.nlm.nih.gov/books/NBK92777/.

Holland, Kimberly. "Amygdala Hijack: What It Is, Why It Happens & How to Make It Stop." *Healthline Media*, 16 Mar. 2023, www.healthline.com/ health/stress/amygdala-hijack#prevention.

Institute of Medicine (US) and National Research Council (US) Committee on the Science of Adolescence. "Biobehavioral Processes." *The Science of Adolescent Risk-Taking: Workshop Report*, U.S. National Library of Medicine, 1 Jan. 1970, www.ncbi.nlm.nih.gov/books/ NBK53414/.

Jensen, Eric P., and Liesl McConchie. *Brain-Based Learning: Teaching the Way Students Really Learn*. SAGE Publications. Kindle Edition, pp. 65–66.

Keirn, Andrea. "Leveraging the Science Behind the Middle School Brain in Your Teaching Strategies." *AMLE*, 5 Apr. 2021, www.amle.org/ leveraging-the-science-behind-the-middle-school-brain-in-your -teaching-strategies/.

MacNabb, Carrie et al. "Neuroscience in Middle Schools: A Professional Development and Resource Program That Models Inquiry-Based Strategies and Engages Teachers in Classroom Implementation." *CBE Life Sciences Education*, U.S. National Library of Medicine, 2006, www.ncbi.nlm.nih.gov/pmc/articles/PMC1618517/.

Reyna, V. F., & Farley, F. "Risk and Rationality in Adolescent Decision Making: Implications for Theory, Practice, and Public Policy." *Psychological Science in the Public Interest*, vol. 7, no. 1, 2006, pp. 1–44. https://doi .org/10.1111/j.1529-1006.2006.00026.x.

Riedijk, Larisa, and Zeena Harakeh. "Imitating the Risky Decision-Making of Peers: An Experimental Study among Emerging Adults." *Emerging Adulthood (Print)*, U.S. National Library of Medicine, Aug. 2018, www .ncbi.nlm.nih.gov/pmc/articles/PMC6195170/.

Robinson, Rebecca. *Implications for Middle Schools from Adolescent Brain Research*. American Secondary Education, 2017. Accessed 25 Apr. 2024.

Semrud-Clikeman, Margaret. "Research in Brain Function and Learning." *American Psychological Association*, www.apa.org/education-career /k12/brain-function. Accessed 25 Apr. 2024.

Scott, Hannah K. "Piaget." *StatPearls [Internet]*, U.S. National Library of Medicine, 9 Jan. 2023, www.ncbi.nlm.nih.gov/books/NBK448206/.

Shapiro, Jeremy. "Two Parts of the Brain Govern Much of Mental Life." *Psychology Today*, Sussex Publishers, May 2021, www .psychologytoday.com/us/blog/thinking-in-black-white-and-gray /202111/two-parts-the-brain-govern-much-mental-life#:~:text=The %20prefrontal%20cortex%20thinks%20relatively,its%20operation %20is%20mostly%20unconscious.

Wheaton, Anne. "Short Sleep Duration among Middle School and High School Students – United States, 2015." *Centers for Disease Control and Prevention*, Centers for Disease Control and Prevention, 25 Jan. 2018, www.cdc.gov/mmwr/volumes/67/wr/mm6703a1.htm?s_cid =mm6703a1_e.

Wilcox, Gabrielle et al. "Why Educational Neuroscience Needs Educational and School Psychology to Effectively Translate Neuroscience to Educational Practice." *Frontiers*, 21 Dec. 2020, www.frontiersin.org/ articles/10.3389/fpsyg.2020.618449/full.

Wolpert-Gawron, Heather. "The Mind of a Middle Schooler: How Brains Learn." *Edutopia*, George Lucas Educational Foundation, 30 Oct. 2013, www.edutopia.org/blog/middle-schooler-mind-how-brains -learn-heather-wolpert-gawron.

Chapter 3: It's Time for Identity Exploration

Fisher, Julia Freeland, and Amy Anderson. "Extracurriculars Are More than Nice-to-Have: They're Essential – Edsurge News." *EdSurge*, EdSurge.com, 25 Apr. 2019, www.edsurge.com/news/2019-04-24 -extracurriculars-are-more-than-nice-to-have-they-re-essential.

Hubley, John et al. *Everybody Rides the Carousel*. 1975.

Kurt, Dr. Serhat. "Vygotsky's Zone of Proximal Development and Scaffolding." *Educational Technology*, 18 Aug. 2020, educationaltech nology.net/vygotskys-zone-of-proximal-development-and-scaffo lding/.

McLeod, Saul et al. "Erikson's Stages of Development." *Simply Psychology*, 25 Jan. 2024, www.simplypsychology.org/erik-erikson.html.

Orenstein, Gabriel A. "Eriksons Stages of Psychosocial Development." *StatPearls [Internet]*, U.S. National Library of Medicine, 7 Nov. 2022, www.ncbi.nlm.nih.gov/books/NBK556096/.

Chapter 4: The Changing Social Dynamics of Middle School

Anthony, Michelle. "Cognitive Development in 11–13 Year Olds." *Scholastic, Scholastic Parents*, 7 Dec. 2018, www.scholastic.com/parents/family -life/creativity-and-critical-thinking/development-milestones/ cognitive-development-11-13-year-olds.html.

Bélanger, Félix et al. "Student Engagement as a Mediator Process between Peer Victimization and Achievement at the Beginning of Middle School." *Journal of School Health*, vol. 93, no. 11, Aug. 2023, pp. 973–981, https://doi.org/10.1111/josh.13388.

Cornwall, Gail. "How Understanding Middle School Friendships Can Help Students with Ups and Downs." *MindShift*, 4 Dec. 2020, www .kqed.org/mindshift/57010/how-understanding-middle-school -friendships-can-help-students.

Damour Ph.D., Lisa. *The Emotional Lives of Teenagers: Raising Connected, Capable, and Compassionate Adolescents*. Random House Publishing Group. Kindle Edition, p. 61.

Johnson, David W. et al. "Cooperative Learning in Middle Schools: Interrelationship of Relationships and Achievement." *Middle Grades Research Journal*, vol. 5, no. 1, 18 Mar. 2010, pp. 1–18, https://doi.org/ ISSN-1937-0814.

Wiseman, Rosalind. *Owning Up: Empowering Adolescents to Create Cultures of Dignity and Confront Social Cruelty and Injustice*. SAGE Publications. Kindle Edition, p. 1.

Chapter 5: The Roles of Grown-Ups in the Middle Grades

"APA Dictionary of Psychology." *American Psychological Association*, dictionary.apa.org/secure-attachment. Accessed 15 May 2024.

"Fentanyl Awareness." *Greene Middle School*, greene.pausd.org/school-life /fentanyl-awareness#:~:text=Fentanyl%20is%20odorless%2C%20 tasteless%20and,manufactured%20by%20a%20pharmaceutical%2 0company. Accessed 30 Apr. 2024.

Ginsburg, Kenneth R. *Congrats – You're Having a Teen!: Strengthen Your Family and Raise a Good Person.* American Academy of Pediatrics, 2023.

Holland, Kimberly. "Amygdala Hijack: What It Is, Why It Happens & How to Make It Stop." *Healthline Media*, 16 Mar. 2023, www.healthline.com/health/stress/amygdala-hijack#prevention.

Holman, Rebecca. "Why Is Parenting So Much Harder Now Than It Was for Our Parents?" *Grazia*, 19 Dec. 2022, graziadaily.co.uk/life/parenting/why-is-parenting-so-much-harder-now-than-it-was-for-our-parents/.

Murthy, Vivek H. "Parental Mental Health & Well-Being." *HHS.Gov*, Office of the Surgeon General, 28 Aug. 2024, www.hhs.gov/surgeongeneral/priorities/parents/index.html.

Neufeld, Gordon, and Gabor Maté. *Hold On to Your Kids: Why Parents Need to Matter More Than Peers.* Random House Publishing Group. Kindle Edition, p. 53.

"Today's Parents Spend More Time with Their Kids Than Moms and Dads Did 50 Years Ago." *UCI News*, 28 Sept. 2016, news.uci.edu/2016/09/28/todays-parents-spend-more-time-with-their-kids-than-moms-and-dads-did-50-years-ago/.

Wolpert-Gawron, Heather. "The Mind of a Middle Schooler: How Brains Learn." *Edutopia*, George Lucas Educational Foundation, 30 Oct. 2013, www.edutopia.org/blog/middle-schooler-mind-how-brains-learn-heather-wolpert-gawron.

Yerkes, Mara A. et al. "In the Best Interests of Children? the Paradox of Intensive Parenting and Children's Health." *Critical Public Health*, vol. 31, no. 3, 27 Nov. 2019, pp. 349–360, https://doi.org/10.1080/09581596.2019.1690632.

Chapter 6: Academics and Middle School: A New Frontier

"12 Recommendations for Middle Grades Success." *12 Recommendations for Middle Grades Success – Middle Grades (CA Dept of Education)*, www.cde.ca.gov/ci/gs/mg/tcsii-12recs.asp. Accessed 30 Apr. 2024.

Anthony, Michelle. "Academic Learning among 11–13 Year Olds." *Scholastic*, Scholastic Parents, 7 Dec. 2018, www.scholastic.com/parents/family-life/creativity-and-critical-thinking/development-milestones/academic-learning-among-11-13-year-olds.html.

Anthony, Michelle. "Cognitive Development in 11–13 Year Olds." *Scholastic*, Scholastic Parents, 7 Dec. 2018, www.scholastic.com/parents/family-life/creativity-and-critical-thinking/development-milestones/cognitive-development-11-13-year-olds.html.

Arulselvi, Evangelin. "Mind Maps in Classroom Teaching and Learning." *Excellence in Education Journal*, vol. 6, no. 2, 2017, pp. 50–65.

Caldarella, Paul et al. "Behavior Monitoring in the Middle Grades: Evaluation of the Classroom Performance Survey." *RMLE Online*, vol. 45, no. 6, 17 May 2022, pp. 1–15, https://doi.org/10.1080/19404476.2022.2073152.

Cumming, Michelle M. et al. "Addressing Middle Schoolers' Disruptive Behavior: The Importance of Fostering Student Executive Functioning." *TEACHING Exceptional Children*, vol. 55, no. 3, 28 Apr. 2022, pp. 176–187, https://doi.org/10.1177/00400599221093393.

Cummings, Emerine L. et al. "Do Not Forget the Keyword Method: Learning Educational Content with Arbitrary Associations." *Journal of Applied Research in Memory and Cognition*, vol. 12, no. 1, Mar. 2023, pp. 70–81, https://doi.org/10.1037/mac0000031.

"Executive Function." *Psychology Today*, Sussex Publishers, www.psychologytoday.com/us/basics/executive-function. Accessed 2 May 2024.

Garey, Juliann. "How Schools Can Support Neurodiverse Students." *Child Mind Institute*, 23 Aug. 2023, childmind.org/article/how-schools-can-support-neurodiverse-students/.

Gonzalez, Jennifer. "8 Things I Know for Sure about (Most) Middle School Kids." *Cult of Pedagogy*, 8 June 2021, www.cultofpedagogy.com/middle-school-kids/.

Jacobson, Lisa A. et al. "The Role of Executive Function in Children's Competent Adjustment to Middle School." *Child Neuropsychology: A Journal on Normal and Abnormal Development in Childhood and Adolescence*, U.S. National Library of Medicine, 2011, www.ncbi.nlm.nih.gov/pmc/articles/PMC4075458/.

Kelleher, Ian. "Teaching Students to Use Evidence-Based Studying Strategies." *Edutopia*, George Lucas Educational Foundation, 5 Oct. 2022, www.edutopia.org/article/teaching-students-use-evidence-based-studying-strategies/.

Lemberger, Matthew E. et al. "Effects of the Student Success Skills Program on Executive Functioning Skills, Feelings of Connectedness, and Academic Achievement in a Predominantly Hispanic, Low-income Middle School District." *Journal of Counseling & Development*, vol. 93, no. 1, Jan. 2015, pp. 25–37, https://doi.org/10.1002/j.1556 -6676.2015.00178.x.

Lemley, Stephanie M. et al. "Metacognition and Middle Grade Mathematics Teachers: Supporting Productive Struggle." *The Clearing House: A Journal of Educational Strategies, Issues and Ideas*, vol. 92, no. 1–2, 9 Jan. 2019, pp. 15–22, https://doi.org/10.1080/00098655.2018.1547264.

McNulty, Laurie Chaikind. *Focus & Thrive: Executive Functioning Strategies for Teens: Tools to Get Organized, Plan Ahead, and Achieve Your Goals.* Rockridge Press, 2020.

Pickhardt, Carl E. "Parenting through the Middle-School Motivation Loss." *Psychology Today*, Sussex Publishers, www.psychologytoday.com /us/blog/surviving-your-childs-adolescence/201910/parenting -through-the-middle-school-motivation-loss. Accessed 2 May 2024.

Ruiz, Elsa Cantú. "Setting Higher Expectations: Motivating Middle Graders to Succeed." *AMLE*, 13 Apr. 2020, www.amle.org/setting-higher -expectations-motivating-middle-graders-to-succeed/.

Schneider, Maryia M. et al. "Middle School Students' Preferences for Praise." *Psychology in the Schools*, vol. 58, no. 2, 6 July 2020, pp. 221– 234, https://doi.org/10.1002/pits.22411.

Sparks, Sarah D. "4 Ways Schools Help or Hinder Gifted Students." *Education Week*, 3 Dec. 2020, www.edweek.org/leadership/4-ways -schools-help-or-hinder-gifted-students/2019/04.

Smith, Megan, and Yana Weinstein. "Learn How to Study Using... Retrieval Practice." *The Learning Scientists*, 10 Feb. 2019, www.learningscientists .org/blog/2016/6/23-1.

Stanford. "Differentiated Instruction." *Center for Teaching and Learning*, ctl .stanford.edu/differentiated-instruction#:~:text=Differentiated%20i nstruction%20involves%20teaching%20in,content%2C%20activit ies%2C%20and%20assessments. Accessed 2 May 2024.

Stanton, Julie Dangremond et al. "Fostering Metacognition to Support Student Learning and Performance." *CBE Life Sciences Education*, U.S. National Library of Medicine, June 2021, www.ncbi.nlm.nih.gov/ pmc/articles/PMC8734377/.

Tahmaseb, Ryan. "How to Support Twice-Exceptional Students." *Edutopia*, George Lucas Educational Foundation, 9 Nov. 2023, www.edutopia .org/article/how-support-twice-exceptional-students/.

Wills, Howard P. et al. "Improving Student Behavior in Middle Schools: Results of a Classroom Management Intervention." *Journal of Positive Behavior Interventions*, vol. 21, no. 4, 2 July 2019, pp. 213–227, https:// doi.org/10.1177/1098300719857185.

Chapter 7: Our Collective Challenge: Technology, Social Media, and the Middle Grades

Barlett, Christopher P. et al. "Predicting Cyberbullying from Anonymity." *Psychology of Popular Media Culture*, vol. 5, no. 2, Apr. 2016, pp. 171– 180, https://doi.org/10.1037/ppm0000055.

boyd, Danah. *It's Complicated: The Social Lives of Networked Teens.* Yale UP, 2015.

CommonSense Education. "Identifying High-Quality Sites Lesson Plan: Common Sense Education." *PBS LearningMedia*, 15 Feb. 2021, ca.pb slearningmedia.org/resource/nmlit17-ela-idhqsites/lesson-plan-ide ntifying-high-quality-sites/#support-materials.

Culotta, Richard. "S5 Episode 1: Digital for Good Raising Kids to Thrive Online." *S5 Episode 1: Digital For Good Raising Kids to Thrive Online*, 20 Sept. 2022, www.healthyscreenhabits.org/s5-episode-1-digital-for -good-raising-kids-to-thrive-in-an-online-world-richard-culatta.

Dawson, Joe. "Who Is That? The Study of Anonymity and Behavior." *Association for Psychological Science – APS*, 30 Mar. 2018, www.psychol ogicalscience.org/observer/who-is-that-the-study-of-anonymity -and-behavior#:~:text=A%202016%20study%20led%20by,positive %20attitudes%20toward%20cyberbullying%20(e.g.%20".

Gill, Rosalind. "Changing the Perfect Picture: Smartphones, Social Media and Appearance Pressures." *Academia.Edu*, 12 Oct. 2021, www.academia.edu/57355738/Changing_the_perfect_picture _Smartphones_social_media_and_appearance_pressures.

Grose, Jessica. "Screens Are Everywhere in Schools. Do They Actually Help Kids Learn?" *The New York Times*, 27 Mar. 2024, www.nytimes .com/2024/03/27/opinion/schools-technology.html?searchResul tPosition=21.

Haidt, Jonathan. "Get Phones out of Schools Now." *The Atlantic*, Atlantic Media Company, 14 June 2023, www.theatlantic.com/ideas/archive/2023/06/ban-smartphones-phone-free-schools-social-media/674304/.

Haidt, Jonathan. *The Anxious Generation: How the Great Rewiring of Childhood Is Causing an Epidemic of Mental Illness*. Penguin Publishing Group. Kindle Edition, 2024, p. 5.

Heitner, Devorah. *Growing Up in Public: Coming of Age in a Digital World* (p. 33). Penguin Publishing Group. Kindle Edition.

Hermans, Anne-Mette et al. "Follow, Filter, Filler? Social Media Usage and Cosmetic Procedure Intention, Acceptance, and Normalization among Young Adults." *Body Image*, vol. 43, Dec. 2022, pp. 440–449, https://doi.org/10.1016/j.bodyim.2022.10.004.

Jacobson, Rae. "Social Media and Self-Doubt." *Child Mind Institute*, 8 Mar. 2024, childmind.org/article/social-media-and-self-doubt/.

Kelly, Yvonne et al. "Social Media Use and Adolescent Mental Health: Findings from the UK Millennium Cohort Study." *EClinicalMedicine*, vol. 6, Dec. 2018, pp. 59–68, https://doi.org/10.1016/j.eclinm.2018.12.005.

Lozano-Blasco, Raquel et al. "Screen Addicts: A Meta-analysis of Internet Addiction in Adolescence." *Children and Youth Services Review*, vol. 135, Apr. 2022, p. 106373, https://doi.org/10.1016/j.childyouth.2022.106373.

Mastruserio, Jennifer. "Parenting in the Digital Era: Setting Boundaries for Screen Time." *Pediatric and Adolescent Medicine*, 14 Nov. 2023, www.pediatricandadolescentmedicine.net/About-Us/Blog/November-2023/screen-time-boundaries-for-children.

McLaughlin, Katie A., and Kevin King. "Developmental Trajectories of Anxiety and Depression in Early Adolescence." *Journal of Abnormal Child Psychology*, vol. 43, no. 2, 6 July 2014, pp. 311–323, https://doi.org/10.1007/s10802-014-9898-1.

Schiffer, Zoe. "Inside the Debate over the Anxious Generation." *Platformer*, Platformer, 12 Apr. 2024, www.platformer.news/anxious-generation-jonathan-haidt-debate-critique/.

Soldatova, Galina et al. "Features of Media Multitasking in School-Age Children." *Behavioral Sciences (Basel, Switzerland)*, U.S. National Library of Medicine, 27 Nov. 2019, www.ncbi.nlm.nih.gov/pmc/articles/PMC6960499/.

Thai, Helen et al. "Reducing Social Media Use Improves Appearance and Weight Esteem in Youth with Emotional Distress." *Psychology of Popular Media*, vol. 13, no. 1, Jan. 2024, pp. 162–169, https://doi.org/10.1037/ppm0000460.

Twenge, Jean M., and Brian H. Spitzberg. "Declines in Non-digital Social Interaction among Americans, 2003–2017." *Journal of Applied Social Psychology*, vol. 50, no. 6, 10 Apr. 2020, pp. 363–367, https://doi.org/10.1111/jasp.12665.

Upton-Clark, Eve. "Gen Z's New Status Symbol." *Business Insider*, www.businessinsider.com/botox-injections-fillers-plastic-surgery-gen-z-social-media-filters-2024-5. Accessed 3 May 2024.

Williams, Mary Elizabeth. "We're Still Way Too Afraid of 'Stranger Danger.'" *Salon*, Salon.com, 3 Feb. 2023, www.salon.com/2023/02/05/were-still-way-too-afraid-of-stranger-danger/.

Chapter 8: Good People Who Do Good Things

Bridgeland, John M. et al. "Engaged for Success: Service-Learning as a Tool for High School Dropout Prevention." *Civic Enterprises*, Civic Enterprises, LLC. 1828 L Street NW 11th Floor, Washington, DC 20036. 2008.

Brown, Tim. "IDEO Design Thinking." *IDEO*, designthinking.ideo.com/. Accessed 3 May 2024.

Gonzalez, Jennifer. "A Collection of Resources for Teaching Social Justice." *Cult of Pedagogy*, 10 Feb. 2023, www.cultofpedagogy.com/social-justice-resources/.

Mcleod, Saul et al. "Kohlberg's Stages of Moral Development." *Simply Psychology*, 17 Jan. 2024, www.simplypsychology.org/kohlberg.html.

Robinson, Rebecca. *Implications for Middle Schools from Adolescent Brain Research*. American Secondary Education, 2017. Accessed 25 Apr. 2024.

Schukar, Ron. "Enhancing the Middle School Curriculum through Service Learning." *Theory Into Practice*, vol. 36, no. 3, June 1997, pp. 176–83, https://doi.org/10.1080/00405849709543765.

"What Is PBL?" *PBLWorks*, Buck Institute for Education, www.pblworks.org/what-is-pbl. Accessed 3 May 2024.

Wolpert-Gawron, Heather. "What the Heck Is Service Learning?" *Edutopia*, George Lucas Educational Foundation, 7 Nov. 2016, www.edutopia.org/blog/what-heck-service-learning-heather-wolpert-gawron.

Printed in the United States
by Baker & Taylor Publisher Services